HERE IS YOUR HOBBY:

Indian Dancing and Costumes

Beginning with a background on Indian dancing, the author then leads you through easy and logical dance stages that include step-by-step photographs. You learn fundamental steps and basic body movements, and discover the importance of chanting and drumming. Next, you learn the advanced steps, including the spectacular hoop dance. The author then includes the important do's and don'ts for assembling authentic Indian costumes, and hints on how to stage a powwow.

HERE IS YOUR HOBBY:

Indian Dancing and Costumes

by
WILLIAM K. POWERS

G. P. Putnam's Sons   **New York**

For Marla, Jeffrey, and Gregory.

Acknowledgments

I would like to thank the following people for their assistance in making this book possible: Paul Theisz, James L. Jeffrey, and Bettye Lane for their fine photographic work; Ronnie Theisz of the Medicine Drum Dancers, New York City, and Jimmy Clark, Wiyaka Dancers, Hornell, New York, for posing for many of the photographs; and all my Indian friends— especially the late John Colhoff (White Man Stands in Sight), Frank Afraid of Horses, the Red Clouds, Bill Horn Cloud, and Henry White Calf, all Sioux from the Pine Ridge Indian Reservation in South Dakota; Paul Thomas, Wichita; the Wahkinney family, Comanche, from Oklahoma; Anthony Marchetta, New Brunswick, New Jersey; and Marlene Rossi, Johnstown, New York.

Pilamayaye,

W.K.P.

Contents

I Dancing Indian   11

II The Hobby   14

III Sing and Drumming   17

IV Basic Body Movements   23

V Basic Steps   30

VI Old-Time Dancing   36

VII Fancy Dancing   42

VIII Fancy-Dance Variation   46

IX The War Dance   56

X The Round Dance   63

XI The Two-Step   68

XII The Scout Dance   72

XIII The Flag Dance   75

XIV The Shield Dance   78

XV The Snake Dance   81

XVI The Buffalo Dance   84

XVII The Stomp Dance   88

XVIII The Hoop Dance   96

XIX Costuming   103

XX The Dance Area   109

XXI How to Run a Powwow   114

XXII Sources of Information   120

Index   125

HERE IS YOUR HOBBY:

Indian Dancing
and Costumes

Young Cheyenne war-dancers at the 1963 Crow Indian Fair at Crow Agency, Montana. They are wearing typical fancy-dance costumes, which are also popular in Oklahoma. (Photo: Jim Jeffrey.)

I

Dancing Indian

Many years have passed since the American Indian donned his buckskin moccasins, breechcloth, and blanket, and strode from his painted tipi to hunt for buffalo, or seek vengeance against a tribal enemy. Eighty years and more have passed since General Custer met his downfall at Little Big Horn, and over seventy years have gone by since the last official battle was fought between the United States Government and the Sioux at Wounded Knee, South Dakota. But the spirit of the American Indian is far from dead.

In these modern times, midst launching space capsules around the earth, beaming television across the ocean, and marveling at the developments of the atomic age, it is difficult to imagine these once mighty hunters and warriors surviving at all.

Occasionally you read about new achievements in Indian education or see a band of "howling redskins" attacking Fort Television. But few of us think of the American Indian as a twentieth-century person living in a separate society with customs different from those of his white brother.

Although the American Indian has resigned himself to wearing Whiteman clothing, working in Whiteman factories, and attending Whiteman schools, he has not forgotten the traditions of his forefathers. During the last twenty years, the Indian has become more interested in his own culture than ever before. Throughout the year, drums boom, singers send forth their songs in high, raspy voices, and thousands of men, women and children adorn themselves in colorful costumes and "dance Indian." To them, celebrating Indian-style represents the old way of life. As summer approaches, the ways of the Whiteman are temporarily forgotten, and powwow fever sweeps the tribes.

The American Indian Exposition in late summer at Anadarko, Oklahoma, is a famous powwow. Here, representatives of thirty-five tribes join together for a week of dancing and visiting friends. The Exposition, called the "Fair" by the Oklahoma Indians, is produced by an all-Indian association and attracts tourists from all parts of the world. Equally popular are the Inter-Tribal Ceremonial at Gallup, New Mexico. Indians from all over the country go there to demonstrate to Indian and non-Indian tourists, the music, dances, and craftwork of their tribes. The Fair and the Ceremonials are scheduled so that Indians may travel from one to the other. This gives more participants an opportunity to compete at both championship war-dance contests, in which young Indian bucks can make a name for themselves and win big cash prizes. Awards are also given, to both men and women, for the best handicraft.

In some other parts of the United States and Canada, Indian celebrations are just as popular. In August, thousands of Indians flock to the Sioux Sun Dance at Pine Ridge, South Dakota. There, for the past five years, the Sioux have danced this religious ceremonial, complete with self-torture, fasting, and long hours of meditation, just as the Sioux did it one hundred years ago. The ceremonial is combined with social dancing in which all tribes are invited to join.

In the summer of 1962, I saw over six hundred men and women dancing in a pine-covered sun-dance arbor. Thousands more traveled from as far north as Canada and as far south as Texas to see and participate in the Sioux celebration.

Other all-Indian celebrations include the Crow Indian Fair at Crow Agency, Montana; Fort Qu'Appelle celebrations at Fort Qu'Appelle, Saskatchewan; All-American Indian Days at Sheridan, Wyoming; Mesquakie Indian Powwow at Tama, Iowa; Chippewa Powwows and pageant at Wisconsin Dells, Wisconsin; Council Fires of the Iroquois in upstate New York; Plaza dances of the Pueblos in New Mexico; and numerous tribal powwows of the Pawnee, Kiowa, Comanche, Ponca, Oto, Osage, and other Oklahoma tribes. On practically all Indian reservations, you can see some form of annual celebrations and weekend powwows.

Many dances are held in conjunction with rodeos and state fairs. At the Pendleton Roundup in Oregon and the Frontier Days in Cheyenne, Wyoming, hundreds of Indians from many tribes are hired to lend exciting atmosphere to the Western events. But these dances are strictly for show. They give Indians an opportunity to travel and meet dancers from other tribes, but they little resemble a true Indian celebration.

Between performances, Indians spend their leisure time visiting each other's campsites, trading, and swapping songs. Song swapping is a favorite pastime.

At night, when the shows are over and the spectators have left the grandstand, the Indians gather in the empty stadium or fairgrounds and dance for their own amusement. Here, the fancy "show" dancing gives way to the round dances, rabbit dances, forty-nines, the partner dances of the Indians. Costumes are replaced with western-style clothing. Except for the strange patterns of dancing and the exotic sounds of the drum and singers, the dancers might be taking part in an old-fashioned square dance. These informal dances begin in the darkness of the night, and they hardly ever end before the sun comes up.

The "powwow circuit" begins in late May and continues through September. Although some celebrations take place during the Christmas holidays, the warm months are for dancing. When the first warm air of Spring is felt, the Indian people begin to gather their feathers and beadwork, buckskin and bells, and prepare for the oncoming season. It is then that the moccasin telegraph sends out the first invitation to dance Indian.

II

The Hobby

While the Indians are demonstrating renewed interest in their own culture, more and more non-Indians are taking up the hobby of Indian dancing. For years, many experts have said that Indian dancing is a wonderful form of exercise. But this Indian hobby offers more than just physical fitness. It also teaches you about the culture of another people.

This knowledge has led many hobbyists to enter related professions and businesses. Among these are anthropology, ethnology, archeology, sociology, museum and library work, teaching, writing, field work for the Bureau of Indian Affairs, and owning private Indian curio shops and mail-order businesses.

Several names have been applied to the hobby of studying Indian culture, but Indian buffs disagree on just what to call the hobby. "Indian lore" has sufficed for many, but others feel that the hobby deserves a more sophisticated name. Names such as "Indian hobbyist," "Indian enthusiast," and "Indianologist" are used to describe persons with various degrees of interest in the Indian.

Perhaps the difficulty in finding the right name is that there are so many facets to the hobby. Some hobbyists are craftsmen; others specialize in collecting. Collectors may have specialties such as arrowheads, books, costume pieces, Katchina dolls, or weapons. Other hobbyists are more scholarly and prefer to study Indian languages, music, history, and religions. Two things that most hobbyists have in common, however, are the owning of an Indian costume and a liking for attending powwows. (The word "powwow" indicates a gathering of hobbyists—usually for a weekend — during which they wear Indian costumes, sing and dance Indian, and trade.)

Once a hobbyist attends a powwow, hears the Indian drum, and sees the rest of the people dancing, chances are — whether he is a professor of anthropology or a Cub Scout — that he'll have a hard time sitting on the sidelines. Sooner or later, he'll be in the dance area stomping it up with the rest.

The hard core of the hobby is "the group," sometimes called a dance club, or dance team. These groups are scattered across the country, but usually band together under such unusual names as the Eastern States Powwow Association, The Monroe Powwow Committee, or the New Jersey Homecoming Powwow Association, for the purpose of putting on Indian-style powwows to which all groups in the region are invited. At these powwows, hundreds of non-Indians (although nowadays many Indians also attend) pack their cars and trailers with camping gear and costumes and spend a weekend dancing Indian. Most of the powwow associations hire Indians to provide the singing.

The purpose of the powwow is not to put on shows for spectators (although visitors are always welcome) but to dance for the pure enjoyment of it. At one time, the hobby was of interest primarily to men and boys. But more and more young women and girls are becoming interested in Indian costumes and dancing. In fact, there are now many coed groups that spend their time studying and enjoying Indian culture.

The hobby has no age limit, and many of the young men who became interested in Indians fifty years ago are still active dancers. In Europe, the Indian hobby often is a pastime for middle-aged people.

Indian powwows are usually near large cities; most of the groups are in metropolitan areas. Football fields, arenas, country estates — anywhere that there is a good surface for dancing — provide a good place for a powwow.

The best way to get started in the Indian hobby is by studying one tribe. Your librarian can help you find appropriate books. Visit your local museums and study designs, colors, and tech-

Hobbyists dancing the war-dance at a powwow. This is the Monroe Powwow, held during the last weekend in June.

niques of making costumes. The last chapter of this book lists the most authoritative references on Indians.

The following pages are written especially for those of you who want to participate in Indian celebrations. Many of the dances, though, are also perfect for school presentations and camp programs. Descriptions of Indian costumes, singing, and history are offered, but the emphasis is on Indian *dancing*.

You may be surprised to discover that nearly half of the dances described are danced by Indians in "street clothes," with no feathered costumes necessary. All of the dances were taught to me by Indians over the past twenty years.

If you follow the book closely, you'll be ready to hit the powwow trail, and there you'll find a host of new friends anxious to help you enjoy the hobby. For those of you just beginning in the hobby, welcome to a whole new world of adventure. Read on, and then, as the Sioux say, "Wiyuškinyan waci po." Dance rejoicedly!

16

III

Sing and Drumming

In the Southwest, a Navajo sings to the rhythm of his horse's hoofs as he rides along. At home, his wife sings a soft lullaby to her son. In the Pueblo villages nearby, a silversmith fashions age-old designs in silver as his hammer taps out the rhythm of the song he sings. In the Florida Everglades, a group of Seminoles sings a vigorous song as they perform the Hunting Dance. In the north woods, a Chippewa sings a sacred song as he prays to Gitche Manito. In the olden days, a Sioux sang a death chant as he rode into battle.

The Indian courts his woman with a love song, cures his sick with a medicine song, and names his children with an honor song. He never ceases to sing whether happy or sad, young or old, well or ailing. From birth to death, the Indian sings.

Indians can sing without dancing, but they cannot dance until they hear an appropriate song. Would you dare get up to dance without hearing the orchestra play? To the Indian, singing is as much a part of the dance as are the dancer's moccasins and bells. For every dance, there is an appropriate song. No dancer can move while the singers are idle. It is the voices of the men and women that makes the dancers *want* to dance. The dancers hear a good song, and their feet are forced to move. The singers actually *control* the dancers.

The Singers

Indian singers and composers are respected men of the Indian community. While all Indians like to sing, there are professional singers who perform at the celebrations. These singers are paid by the committee that sponsors the dance, or the people donate money to them in a formal "give-away" ceremony. Sometimes the singers receive food or tobacco as payment for their singing.

Songs are passed down from generation to generation. But in addition to these "classical" songs of the old-timers, there are many new songs composed. At the annual celebrations, these new songs make their debut before the people. Some become popular enough to travel from one reservation to the next until people from all tribes are singing them. A new song may remain popular for many years.

The Drums

The drum is the Indians' most popular musical instrument. Some tribes used flutes, whistles, boraches, rattles, and one-string violins, but no other instrument has gained the drum's prominence.

Large dance drum of the Sioux measures up to 33 inches in diameter. It is made from buffalo hides stretched across a wooden frame and laced tightly. (Photo: courtesy of Museum of the American Indian, Heye Foundation.)

Charlie Phillips and Ted Bison, both Sioux Indians from South Dakota, and Louis Garcia of Glen Cove, New York, singing at the New Jersey Indian Homecoming Powwow. Two modern conveniences used by present-day singers are the commercial bass drum and the microphone.

Drums come in various sizes and shapes depending on the tribes that use them. There are large dance drums that range from two to five feet in diameter. Smaller hand drums range from six to eighteen inches in diameter. These drums may have one head or two. Most dance drums are made from cow-, goat-, or deerskin stretched over wood frames. Drum frames, or shells, may be made from a cedar wash tub, hollowed log, metal oil drum, brass kettle, or commercial bass-drum frame. Many of the northern-plains tribes use bass drums.

Drumsticks also vary in length and shape. They should be made from a hard wood such as oak. Many singers nowadays carve their sticks from chair and table legs. The "heads" are made from cotton wrapped with adhesive tape, or buckskin stuffed with cotton and sewn. A makeshift drumstick by tying a Bull-Durham sack filled with grass over one end of a branch half an inch in diameter. Singers who play bass drums prefer to use commercial bass-drum sticks with a soft head.

19

Rhythm

Although the sound of the drum can easily make a dancer want to dance, the drum can never be used as a substitute for singing. *The drum merely accents the rhythm of the song.* Although it is not necessary to have music while learning Indian dancing, it is important to have singing or recorded music as part of your pow-wows or shows.

Indian singing is difficult for some, but the basic drum rhythms are relatively simple. In the dances described in this book, only three totally different rhythms are used. The most important rhythms are:

One-quarter time. This is the most popular drum rhythm, sometimes called the war-dance beat. It can be recognized by its steady, unaccented beat. Although it is most frequently heard in the war-dance, it is also played for the hoop dance, and parts of the sneak-up dance.

The one-quarter beat may be played in three different tempos — slow, medium, and fast. These tempos will be indicated at the beginning of each dance. When you learn the preliminary steps and body movements, practice them slowly first, gradually working up to the proper speed.

The slow one-quarter time is written ♩=120, and indicates that you play 120 beats of the drum per minute. Medium one-quarter time is written ♩=180, indicating 180 beats per minute. And fast one-quarter time is written ♩=320, meaning 320 beats per minute.

Three-quarter time. The rhythm heard next most frequently is three-quarter time. Musicians will recognize this as waltz time. In the Indian version of three-quarter time, however, the second beat is omitted. All that you hear is one–three, one–three. The one–beat is played louder than the three-beat, so three-quarter time beat can readily be identified by its characteristic loud-soft, loud-soft rhythm. It will be written: ♩ ♩.

The three-quarter beat is also played in three distinct tempos.

20

In the rabbit dance, the tempo is $\quarternote=136$. In the round dance, it is slightly faster: $\quarternote=160$. And in the forty-nine, it is even faster: $\quarternote=200$.

To learn how to play the three-quarter beat, simply count to yourself ONE-two-three, ONE-two-three. After you have mastered this, eliminate the two-beat on the drum, and count it to yourself: ONE-(two)-three, ONE-(two)-three.

Thunder-drumming. This is not really a rhythm, but a technique of drumming often used as an introduction to dances. It is heard in the sneak-up dance and buffalo dance. In thunder-drumming, the drum is played very rapidly and sounds much like thunder.

Of the rhythms discussed here, one variation occurs in the buffalo dance. This variation may be called *half-time.* It is really slow one-quarter time played at $\quarternote=60$.

Accented beats. If you listen to Indian records, you can hear accented beats occur irregularly in war-dance, round-dance and rabbit-dance songs. These accented beats are played to keep the dancers in step. Also, if a singer is not beating the drum properly, another singer will hit the drum loudly to make the other aware that he is out of time. This accenting varies among tribes; generally, the Sioux, Crow, Cree, and other tribes of the northern plains accent their drum at least five times during each song. The southern-plains tribes accent their drum beats three times during each song. Among both northern- and southern-plain tribes, the drum beats get louder as the end of the song approaches.

When dancers hear the accented beats, they dip very low, or they turn rapidly. This is called honoring the drum. The dancers in this movement express their happiness at hearing the good songs the singers are singing.

Learning to Sing

While the average hobbyist finds some difficulty in singing

Indian, there are usually a few in the group who are able to reproduce the Indian "sound."

The best way to learn to sing, unless you happen to live near a reservation and can find someone to teach you, is to listen to recordings of Indian music. These can be bought from companies listed in the last chapter.

You'll find that after listening to these records you can begin to pick up the tune of the song. After you've learned your first song, the rest come easily. Most hobbyists find that war-dance songs and round-dance songs are the easiest to learn first.

You can use these records as a substitute for "live" singing while you dance. If you want to dance for a long period, you may wish to record a series of songs on tape.

After you have learned the steps and variations described in Chapter 4 through Chapter 8, try practicing to records. This will greatly add to the atmosphere of the dancing and will give you more feeling for the steps.

IV

Basic Body Movements

In August of 1949, I attended a Sioux celebration at Oglala, South Dakota. About forty dancers were in the dance-shade. Eight singers crowded around a large drum, their piercing voices inspiring the dancers to dance well. Men, women, and children crowded the dance-shade. Despite the 90-degree temperature, everyone was having a good time.

Midway through the day, a new dancer appeared at the shade entrance. He was dressed in black tights, neck and back bustles, and hair roach. His face was painted yellow; blue stripes underlined his eyes. The man — who appeared to be about age forty — gave a few yells and waved to the people. Everyone turned and took note of the newcomer.

Rather than walk into the dance area, the man danced in, shaking his head vigorously to the tempo of the drum, wheeling his body about in beautiful angular motions. What magnificent style!

He was much more agile than the younger dancers; his footwork was fancy, but his body movement resembled that of the older dancers. His body was erect and his back flat through all of his gyrations. Even as he dipped low, bending forward, his back was still flat, his head raised and bobbing in time to the singers' voices and the throbs of the drum.

What made this man's dance movements superior to those of the other dancers? His posture. He was aware of his body movement with every step he took. He did not concentrate only on intricate footwork.

The members of the tribe considered him a true champion dancer.

In all kinds of Indian dancing, body posture is just as important as footwork. Indians judge a dancer by the way he carries himself, the way he uses his head, shoulders, body, and arms. Although the younger generation prefers fast and furious stepping to the traditional easy-flowing movements, the traditional style should not be neglected.

Let's discuss how to use each part of your body separately, and then put these movements together with basic steps.

Posture

Stand erect, with your feet parallel and six to eight inches apart, toes pointing directly forward. Keep your back flat, and relax your shoulders. Your arms should rest normally at your sides.

Left, Anthony Marchetta, 16, of New Brunswick High School, New Brunswick, New Jersey, demonstrates the basic Indian stance (with hands on hips). Right, note that the dancer's head forms a 45-degree angle with his shoulder.

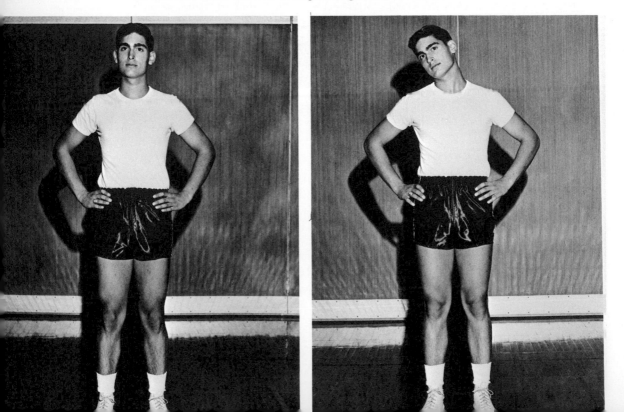

Head

The Indians say that in the old days a good dancer made his crest feathers "wrestle." The crest feathers are inserted into sockets on top of the hair roach so that the feathers twirl freely as the dancer moves his head. As the feathers spin, they slap against each other, resembling two men wrestling. A good dancer makes his feathers wrestle throughout the dance. To do so, he must constantly keep his head shaking up and down, and must move it from side to side and in small circles. Good head movements are among the most beautiful parts of Indian dancing.

Practice these typical head movements:

Shaking. Move your head as if you were shaking it "yes." This is a subtle movement. Don't jerk your head up and down, but move it easily. Relax your neck.

Look to your left. Now begin shaking your head, bringing your chin down on every beat of the drum. As you shake your head, slowly move it to the right so that you end the movement looking over your right shoulder. Repeat the same motions from right to left.

Now try the same simple exercise, only this time bring your chin down *two times* for every beat of the drum. Again move your head from left to right, and back again, until you feel relaxed doing the exercise.

Trembling. Try the shaking exercise again, but this time shake your head very quickly *out of time* with the drum. Your head will appear to be trembling. As in the first exercise, move your head back and forth from left to right, right to left.

Circling. Either shake your head in time with the drum, or let it tremble. At the same time, facing forward, move your head in small circles, as if you had a piece of chalk on your forehead and you were drawing circles on a blackboard.

Other Variations. Again shaking your head, lean it to the left so that your head forms a 45-degree angle with the top of your left shoulder. Slowly move your head so that it leans to the right forming a 45-degree angle with your right shoulder. Repeat this movement over and over until it becomes second nature to you. Now try combining all of the head movements, making sure the transitions are smooth. Be careful not to jerk your head and not to overemphasize the shaking movement. Keep your neck and shoulders relaxed.

Shoulders

Generally, you carry your shoulders normally as in walking. Some Indians, however, like to rotate their shoulders backward as they dance, alternating left and right.

Practice this shoulder movement: Assume the Indian stance with shoulders relaxed. Raise the left shoulder two or three inches. Push your shoulder back as far as it will go, and then lower it back into place. As the left shoulder drops back, raise your right shoulder two or three inches, push it back as far as it will go, and lower it back into place.

Again begin with the left shoulder and repeat the entire exercise until it becomes easy. Remember not to exaggerate the shoulder movements. Each should be a smooth transition, with one shoulder rotating backward after the other.

Among some tribes, the shoulders are sometimes shaken back and forth, alternating left and right. This movement is done very quickly, almost at a tremble. Although it looks foreign to American Indian dancing, it is quite popular among the northern Sioux, Cheyenne, Arapaho, and Cree. This movement is appropriate only when you are wearing a northern grass-dance costume.

Now that you've learned some movements of the head and shoulders, try combining the two. Start out by *shaking* your head in time with the drum and at the same time rotate your shoulders slowly. When you've mastered this, try *trembling* your head, and other variations of the head movements, coupled with the movements of your shoulders.

Torso

Most war dancing is done in an upright position. Your back is flat, and your pelvis is held normally, as in walking. A good dancer avoids sticking out his rump or hunching his back. If his body leans forward, backward, or to one side, his back remains flat. His head is either held up, or in line with his spine.

Arms

The arms may be held at the side, on the hips, or bowed. Old-time dancers prefer the bowed position.

Hands

The hands are relaxed normally, or the fingers are slightly clenched in a fist. Fingers are *always closed, never* rigid or spread apart.

Left, note the relation of the right and left shoulders in the rotating movement. Right, the dancer leans forward with a flat back. Note that his head is held upright.

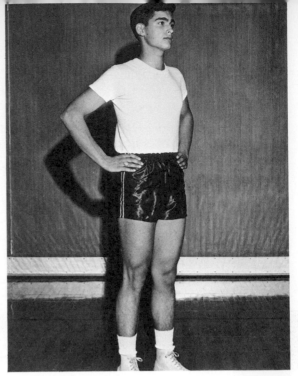

Leaning to the side, the dancer holds his head erect.

Hands on both hips.

Favorite of the old-timers—the bowed position.

One hand on his hip, the other at his side. Note the relaxed hands.

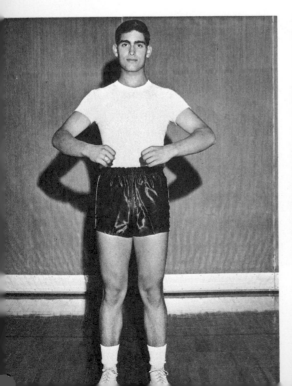

If you hold your hands and arms in the bowed position, keep time with the drum by moving them slightly up and down the way you would if you were scrubbing clothes on an old-fashioned washboard. Don't overemphasize this movement.

Style

Many dancers like to carry fans, bows and arrows, tomahawks, mirror boards, hoops, decorated whistles, or rattles. They use these props as they would be used normally — fanning the fan, feinting with the tomahawk at an imaginary enemy, or shaking the rattle in time with the drum.

Because war-dancing is truly freestyle, there are no restrictions about how the movements of the head, shoulders, body, arms, and hands may be used. It is up to each dancer to combine his movements so they flow smoothly together.

Remember, Indian dancing is not wild, but controlled. Indians dislike watching dancers who overemphasize their steps and body movements. Even in the fastest dances of the southern plains, when the drums beat out rhythms with machine-gun speed, the dancers still control every movement of their feet and bodies.

Once you've learned how to use the basic body movements, it's time to consider the basic steps of Indian dancing.

V

Basic Steps

Once I watched an Indian teach his two very small sons how to dance. As he beat the drum and sang, the two tots hopped and shuffled about the rough floor of the cabin. The man interrupted his song occasionally by calling out to the boys, "Kuciyela!" Bend low! The boys crouched down and shook their heads at the floor. If the boys got in each other's way, the father shouted "Kaablaya po!" Spread out! The boys responded by quickly separating.

During no part of the lesson did the father, in the usual sense of the word, teach his boys how to dance. He didn't tell them how to place their feet or shake their heads. He simply reminded them to change their body positions or directions of dance.

Indian children learn to dance by watching their parents perform. At two or three, the young Indian boy or girl can easily stomp it up with the best of dancers. He responds naturally to the sound of the drums and voices of the singers.

Since most of you do not have access to the Indian method of training, dancing must be thoroughly taught; the steps must be clearly described. Although the Indians do not use names to indicate the different kinds of steps, I have named them for easy reference. After you've learned the steps, you may discard the names if you wish.

The primary purpose of any Indian dance step is to keep time with the drum and song. I cannot overemphasize this. Indians dislike seeing dancers perform fast, intricate steps with no regard for rhythm.

The basic war-dance steps are the most popular among the majority of Indian tribes, so I'll discuss them first.

30

Slow Tap-Step

This is the basic step of Indian dancing. Begin by assuming the Indian stance, feet parallel and separated about six to eight inches. Point your toes directly forward. Avoid dancing either pigeon-toed or with your toes pointing out.

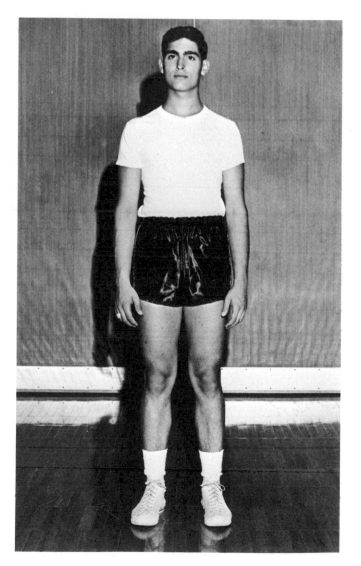

Slow tap dance.

First beat.

Right, on the third beat, step forward on the right foot. The body rises to its normal position.

It takes four beats to perform the complete step:

First beat: Your weight is on your right foot. Tap the ball of your left foot on the ground in front of you so that the arch of your left foot is beside the toe of your right foot. (Photo above.)

Second beat: Place your left foot back in position. Shift the weight of your body to your left foot.

Third beat: Tap your right foot in front of your body, the arch of your right foot even with your left toes. (Photo at right.)

Fourth beat: Place your right foot back into position. Your weight shifts to your right foot, and you are ready to begin the complete step again.

First practice this simple tap-step in place. After you have mastered it, try moving forward using it. As you go forward, your foot is not placed all the way back into position on the second and fourth beats; it comes only halfway back.

When you feel comfortable doing the tap-step, try combining it with the arm, head, and shoulder motions. Move forward while your head shakes in time with the drum. Then try rotating your shoulders.

Third beat.

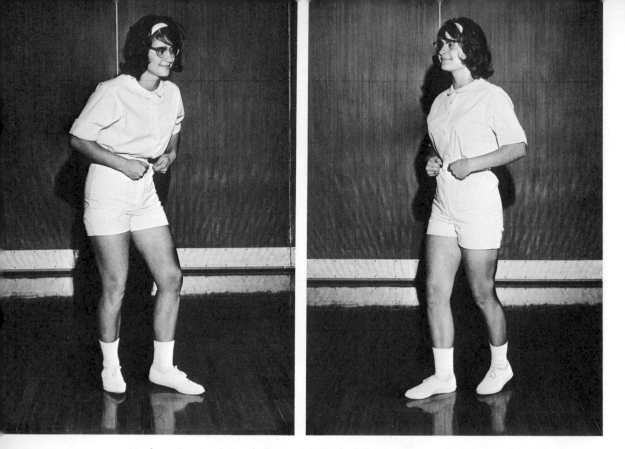

Marlene Rossi, of South Brunswick High School, Monmouth Junction, New Jersey, demonstrates the toe-heel step. On the first beat, step on the ball of the left foot. On the second beat, the heel drops and the body lowers a few inches.

As you combine your head, shoulder, and arm movements with the tap-step, try doing this routine: Dance forward for eight beats. At the eighth beat turn diagonally to your right, and repeat the tap-step for another eight beats. Turn diagonally left for eight beats. Repeat the entire routine.

Now try dancing in about a two-foot circle to your left, then in a circle to your right. After you've practiced circling, try dancing the tap-step in a small figure eight.

Toe-Heel

Assume the Indian stance with feet parallel and six to eight inches apart. The toe-heel is done in four beats:

34

First beat: Your weight is on your right foot. Step on the ball of your left foot. As in the tap-step the arch of your left foot is even with the toes of your right foot.

Second beat: Drop your left heel. As the heel drops, shift the weight of your body to your left foot, and lower your body a few inches.

Third beat: Step on the ball of your right foot. Your body rises to its normal position.

Fourth beat: Drop your right heel. As your heel drops, shift the weight of your body to your right foot and lower your body a few inches.

The shifting of your weight and lowering of your body create a beautiful rise-and-fall movement.

As with the tap-step, try combining the head, shoulder, and arm movements with the toe-heel step. Practice dancing in small circles and figure eights.

Legs

In Indian dancing, your legs should be flexed, bent slightly under the weight of your body. In the tap-step and toe-heel, each time the weight shifts, the body lowers a couple of inches. The "free" leg also is flexed.

There are some exceptions to keeping the legs flexed. Some skilled dancers occasionally like to tap their foot by reaching far out in front of their bodies with the leg held straight and stiff.

As you do this step, your body leans forward, and your back is flat.

After you've practiced combining the footwork with the head, shoulder, and arm movements, you may stop counting the beats and instead change steps and variations on whatever beats you please. The Indians do not count a series of four or eight, as we are accustomed to doing. I've used the counts simply to make it easy for you to learn the steps. After you've practiced the exercises, your only restriction is to *keep in time with the drum.*

VI

Old-Time Dancing

The slow tap-step and toe-heel are the basic steps of the old-time Indians. Dancers usually begin each war-dance with these steps. But after a few minutes "on the floor," dancers may break into any number of step variations, combining these with more tap-steps and toe-heels.

By learning the variations described in this chapter, you can begin to develop your own style of dancing.

Jarring the Heels

A great number of slow war-dance variations are performed by jarring one heel in place, while you tap the ball of the other foot on the ground to the front, side, and behind your body. There are innumerable variations of heel jarring.

Jarring the heels.

First try rising up on the balls of your feet, lifting your heels off the ground a few inches. Now drop your heels. Repeat this over and over, in time to the drum.

Now dance forward, using the slow tap-step for eight beats. Stop and jar your heels in place for four beats. Dance forward again with the slow tap-step. Again stop and jar your heels in place for four beats.

Try the exercise again, jarring your heels only twice between the tap-steps.

Tap-Heel Steps

Assume the Indian stance, feet parallel and separated six to eight inches. Place your arms in the bowed position. Your weight is on the left foot.

First beat: Tap the ball of your right foot in front of your body as if you were beginning the tap-step.
Second beat: Jar the left heel.
Third beat: Tap the ball of your right foot to the side of your body. In this position, your feet are parallel and twelve to fourteen inches apart.
Fourth beat: Jar the left heel.

Repeat again. Then reverse the step, tapping your left foot and jarring your right heel.

Here is another variation:

First beat: Tap your right foot to the side. Feet are parallel, twelve to fourteen inches apart.
Second beat: Jar the left heel.
Third beat: Tap your right toe behind your left foot.
    Fourth beat: Jar your left heel.
    Reverse the step, tapping your left foot and jarring your right heel.

Cross-over Steps

The cross-over steps are similar to the tap-heel steps. The difference, as the name implies, is that the tapping foot crosses the standing foot.

As in the tap-heel steps, you jar one heel as the opposite foot taps across the front of your standing leg, as the accompanying photo shows. Let's call this position 1. The next photo shows how you tap your foot to the front and side of your body. This is position 2. The next photo shows how you cross your foot behind your standing leg. This is position 3. The final photo in the series shows how you tap the ball of one foot to the side and slightly behind your standing leg. This is position 4. Try these positions on both the right side and left side.

Here is an eight-beat exercise using all four positions of the cross-over steps. Assume the Indian stance with your weight on your left foot.

First beat: Tap the ball of your right foot at position 1.
Second beat: Jar your left heel in place.
Third beat: Tap the ball of your right foot at position 2.
Fourth beat: Jar your left heel in place.
Fifth beat: Tap the toe of your right foot at position 3. In this
    position the calves of your legs touch.
Sixth beat: Jar your left heel in place.
Seventh beat: Tap the ball of your right foot at position 4.
Eighth beat: Jar your left heel in place, and begin again.

Try the entire exercise on the other side, tapping the left foot and jarring the right heel.

Push-Turns

Again using the principle of the tap-heel steps, you can turn on one foot as you push yourself around with the other. Try tapping your right foot at position 2. Then jar your left heel; at the same time, move to your left, rotating on the ball of your left foot. Each time you tap your right foot, push yourself slightly, in a circle to your left, on the ball of your left foot. Try the same turn moving in a circle to your right, tapping your left foot and jarring your right heel.

Trots

Sometimes an old-time war-dancer intersperses his tap-steps with trots, simply alternating feet with each beat of the drum for two or three beats. You may trot forward, backward, or to either side. The legs are barely raised off the ground. Practice this:

Dance four tap-steps forward.
Take four trot steps in place.
Dance two tap-steps forward.
Take four trot steps forward.

Try doing this combination of steps in a two-foot circle, first to your right, and then to your left.

Here is an interesting back-and-forth variation of the trot step:

First beat: Step forward on your left foot.
Second beat: Step back on your right foot.
Third beat: Step back on your left foot.
Fourth beat: Step forward on your right foot.

Now reverse.

First beat: Step back on your left foot.
Second beat: Step forward on your right foot.
Third beat: Step forward on your left foot.
Fourth beat: Step back on your right foot.

These trot steps are simple, but when combined with tap-steps and toe-heels, they add an interesting flourish to your dancing.

Position 1. The dancer crosses one foot in front of the other.

Position 2. The dancer taps his foot to the front and side of his body.

Position 3. The dancer crosses his leg and taps his foot behind his standing leg.

Position 4. The dancer taps the ball of one foot to the side and slightly behind his standing leg.

Walking in Time with the Drum

Some old-timers have seen so many winters that their legs are no longer supple enough to perform even the simple tap-steps and toe-heels. They simply walk in time with the drum. As they walk, their bodies lean slightly forward. They usually wear flowing warbonnets and buckskin suits. They may not be able to compete with the younger generation of dancers, but they can enjoy the songs and remember the days of their youth, when they too were nimble of foot. The simple movements of these old-timers are beautiful to watch.

Although the variations of steps presented here are done as exercises, they may actually be done in the slow war-dance. When you have mastered these exercises, try doing them combined with the head, shoulder, and arm movements. Generally, old-timers dance with their hands held in one of three ways: normally at their sides, on their hips, or bowed. Traditionally they carry fans, bows and arrows, tomahawks, pipe bags, and other mementos of the buffalo-hunting days.

Again, these exercises may be practiced to slow war-dance records.

Although slow war-dancing doesn't have the excitement of fast war-dancing, it can be just as enjoyable to perform and watch. Most young Indians agree that no matter how they strut their stuff on the dance floor during the war-dance contests, nothing is more inspiring than to watch old people of their tribe dancing the slow, rhythmic steps so reminiscent of bygone days.

VII

Fancy Dancing

Fancy dancing is a term applied by Indians to a very fast style of war-dancing characterized by quick turns, abrupt changes in body positions, and erratic foot-tapping. This style is the direct opposite of the slow war-dancing described in the previous chapter. Fancy dancing is the dance of the modern generation of American Indians.

The Kiowa, Comanche, Southern Cheyenne and Arapaho, Ponca, and Oto of Oklahoma are the foremost exponents of fancy dancing. Every summer at the American Indian Exposition at Anadarko, Oklahoma, members of these tribes compete against each other for cash prizes and the coveted title, Champion War-Dancer. This kind of dancing has become so popular on the southern plains that even young girls — dressed in men's clothing — compete, right along with the young bucks.

Fast Tap-step

This is the basic step of fancy dancing. It is a combination of the slow tap-step you have already learned, and a hop.

To begin, assume the Indian stance with your feet parallel and separated six to eight inches. Remember, the rules that apply to body posture in slow war-dance steps also hold true for fast dancing. Every movement is *controlled*.

First beat: Your weight is on your right foot. Hop on your right foot and tap your left foot on the ground in front of your body. As in the slow tap-step, the arch of your left foot is even with the toes of your right.

Your weight is on the right foot. Hop on your right foot and tap your left foot on the ground in front of your body.

Hop on your left foot and tap your right foot.

Second beat: Place your left foot back into position, shifting your weight to your left foot.

Third beat: Hop on your left foot and tap your right foot. The arch of your right foot is even with the toe of your left.

Fourth beat: Place your right foot back into position, and you are ready to begin again.

Try doing the fast tap-step slowly first, gradually increasing the speed. As you notice, the only difference between the slow and fast tap-steps is the hop. This hop should not be exaggerated; lift your feet off the ground only slightly. Avoid raising your knees and hopping high off the ground.

If you do the step correctly, the hop of one foot and the tap of the other fall almost exactly on the same beat, the tap following

43

the hop by only a split-second. If you do the step with street shoes on, you can hear a triple beat — hop-tap-step, hop-tap-step (rat-a-tat, rat-a-tat).

Practice the fast tap-step, using the same exercises you did in learning the slow tap-step, moving forward, and in small circles and figure eights.

As with the slow tap-step, there are innumerable variations of the fast tap-step. In very fast dancing, the basic step is combined with trots, tap-heels, cross-overs, and other variations. Most of these variations are accomplished *by hopping on one foot while the free foot performs intricate movements both on and off the ground.* The hopping foot is alternated irregularly, but in time with the drum.

To perform these fancy movements properly, you need a certain amount of conditioning. Here are some exercises that will help you build the muscles in your legs and get accustomed to alternating feet, smoothly.

Begin by hopping on your left foot for sixty-four beats. Then change to your right foot, and hop for sixty-four beats. Change again for thirty-two beats on each foot and then to sixteen, eight, four, and then back to sixty-four beats again. Don't overwork yourself. Give your legs muscles a chance to get accustomed to this rigorous exercise.

You can do this same exercise with the free foot tapping lightly in front of the hopping foot.

Here's an exercise for controlling your free foot. You move your foot behind, around to the side, and in front of your body as you hop on the opposite foot.

First beat: Hop on both feet.
Second beat: Hop on your left foot, and extend your right foot behind.

Third beat: Hop on your left foot, and extend your right foot to the side.

Fourth beat: Hop on your left foot, and extend your right foot in front.

Now try the same exercise hopping on your right foot, extending your left foot to the three positions. Practice this over and over until there is a smooth transition in changing from left to right.

After you have mastered this, try moving in a small circle to your left as you hop on your left foot and extend your right. Then reverse. This teaches you how to alternate feet and change direction simultaneously. As you will see in the next chapter, the alternating of the hopping foot and changing of direction are the key to fancy dancing.

After you feel comfortable doing the exercises in this chapter, and have practiced them to records along with proper head, shoulder and arm movements, you will be ready to go on to the next chapter.

VIII

Fancy-Dance Variation

I have watched champion war-dancers from all parts of the nation compete. Their styles differ somewhat according to their tribes, but they all have certain qualities in common: they keep in time with the drum, end on the last beat of the song, and never move very far away from their own dance spot.

Most dancers, in fact, never move more than a foot or two in any direction. They seem almost nailed to one small area. Instead of covering a lot of territory, they dip low, whirl suddenly, straighten up, and dart their feet unexpectedly in front and behind. The dancer's ability lies not so much in the intricacy of his footwork (although this is the illusion that he creates) as in the change of direction and the sudden rise and fall and abrupt turning. This adds real excitement to the dance!

Since fancy-dance variations largely consist of maneuvering the free foot in intricate patterns while you hop on the opposite foot, we can safely say that fancy-dance variations fall into four categories. They are (1) fast tap-stepping, forwards, backwards, and sideways; (2) turns and pivots; (3) quick steps; and (4) cross-over steps.

We have already learned the fast tap-step in the last chapter, so let us begin with the turns and pivots.

Hop-turns

There are four ways to perform hop-turns:

1. Hopping in a circle to your left on your left foot.
2. Hopping in a circle to your left on your right foot.
3. Hopping in a circle to your right on your right foot.
4. Hopping in a circle to your right on your left foot.

When practicing, the hopping foot hops on every beat of the drum.

46

To get the feel of hop-turns, try the following exercise:

Eight beats: Hop on your left foot and turn in a complete circle to your left.

Eight beats: Hop on your right foot and continue turning to your left for another full turn.

Eight beats: Hop on your right foot and turn in a complete circle to your right.

Eight beats: Hop on your left foot and continue turning to your right for another complete circle.

When doing this exercise, imagine that there is a small spot on the ground. Your hopping foot never goes outside of this spot as you turn. Make the transition from left foot to right foot easily. Your free foot is simply raised off the ground a few inches.

After learning this exercise, try it in half-time, making half-circles.

Four beats: Hop on your left foot, and turn to your left until you have completed a half-circle.

Four beats: Change to hopping on your right foot, and continue turning to your left until you have completed the full circle.

Reverse the exercise.

Now that you've learned to use the hopping foot, let's use the free foot. Note the positions of the feet in the accompanying photos.

In the first photo, the dancer holds his free foot in front of his hopping foot. We will call this position 1. In the second photo, the dancer holds his foot in front and slightly to the side of his opposite foot. This is position 2. In the third photo, he holds his free foot behind the standing leg. This is position 3. And in the fourth photo, the dancer holds his free foot behind and slightly to the

Position 1. The dancer holds his free foot in front of his hopping foot.

Position 2. The dancer holds his foot in front and slightly to the side of his opposite foot.

Position 3. He holds his free foot behind the standing leg.

Position 4. The dancer holds his free foot behind and slightly to the side of his standing leg.

The dancer points his right foot.

The dancer holds his left foot in the flexed position.

side of his standing leg. This is position 4. The free foot may be either pointed or flexed.

Now try all of the hop-turn exercises, only this time place your free foot in one of the four positions. For example . . .

Eight beats: Hop on your left foot, and turn in a complete circle to your left (your right foot is held in position 1) — and so on, for all four positions.

Try the eight-beat and four-beat exercises, each time holding the free foot in a different position, until you feel comfortable doing the turns with the free foot held in any one of the four positions.

After you have practiced these, try doing the hop-turns, this time allowing your free foot to pass through the four positions as you turn in one complete circle. In the first exercise — as you hop on your left foot turning in a complete circle to your left — your right foot passes from position 4 through to position 1 in a graceful motion. You can also do this turn with your right foot starting at position 1 and passing back through to position 4 as you turn to your left.

Using the four kinds of hop-turns, plus the four positions at which the free foot is held, you can work out many different combinations. How easily you change directions of movement, and position of feet — without missing a beat of the drum — partially determines the quality of your dancing style.

To give you an idea of how these variations fit together in a dance, here is a combination of steps and variations, each taking sixty-four beats to complete. Remember, there is no set routine in fancy dancing. This combination is provided so that you may get the feel of changing gracefully from one step to another. After you have become proficient at doing the turns, you may develop your own combination of steps.

To begin this exercise, your weight is on your left foot.

Eight beats: Do four fast tap-steps forward.
Four beats: Hop on your left foot in a half-circle to your left, with your free foot in position 1.
Four beats: Hop on your right foot, completing the circle to your left; your free foot is held in position 1.
Eight beats: Do a fast tap-step in place.
Four beats: Hop on your right foot to your right in a half-circle; your free foot is in position 3.
Four beats: Hop on your left foot, continuing in a half-circle to your right; your right foot is in position 3.
Four beats: Do a fast tap-step in place.
Four beats: Hop on your right foot to your right, completing a full circle; your free foot is in position 2.
Eight beats: Do fast tap-steps in a two-foot circle to your left.
Four beats: Hop on your left foot to your left, completing a full circle; your right foot is in position 2.
Four beats: Do fast tap-steps forward.

50

Four beats: Hop on your left foot in a half-circle to your left; your free foot is in position 1.

Four beats: Hop on your right foot in a half-circle to your right; your free foot is in position 1.

There is no limit to the number of variations you can work out using tap-steps and hop-turns. After you have mastered this exercise, try changing free-foot positions and directions on odd- rather than even-numbered beats.

Pivots

There are two ways in which you can pivot: to your left on your left foot, and to your right on your right foot. The pivot turn is made by whipping the free foot in the direction of the turn while you pivot on the ball of the opposite foot. The free foot begins its whipping movement from position 3 and passes through to position 1 upon completion of the turn. Usually you cannot do more than a half-turn at a time. Pivot turns are an exciting way to lead into hop-turns.

Try pivoting on your left foot to your left. The right foot starts at position 3 and whips around through to position 1. As the momentum of the pivot turn stops, continue around to your left hopping on your left foot. Try this turn, pivoting on your right foot.

Quick Steps

The quick steps described in the slow war-dance chapter are also used in fancy dancing. They are done on the balls of the feet. Some dancers raise their knees very high — more like a football exercise than a variation of Indian dancing. The quick steps may be done frontward, backward, or sideways.

Here is an exercise incorporating the quick steps with pivots and hop-turns.

Pivot on your left foot to your left, with your right foot in position 2. As the momentum stops, do four hop-turns on your left foot, continuing to your left with your right foot in position 1. Do two quick steps, and finish with four tap-steps, still dancing in a circle to your left.

Cross-over Steps

Cross-over steps in fancy dancing are related to cross-over steps in slow war-dancing. The difference is that in fancy dancing you hop on one foot while you tap the free foot in positions 1 through 4. The cross-over exercises given for slow war-dancing apply to fancy dancing.

Cross-over steps may be incorporated in hop-turns. In doing so, tap your free foot in any of the four positions as you turn. Usually the tapping of the free foot is done on *every other* beat, as the opposite foot hops on *every* beat.

Here is an eight-beat exercise to help you practice cross-over steps: Assume the Indian stance, hand on hips.

First beat: Hop on your left foot; at the same time, tap the ball of your right foot at position 1.

Second beat: Hop on your left foot; your right foot moves to position 2, off the ground.

Third beat: Hop on your left foot, and tap the ball of your right foot at position 2.

Fourth beat: Hop on your left foot, and move your right foot to position 3, off the ground.

Fifth beat: Hop on your left foot, and tap the toe of your right foot at position 3.

Sixth beat: Hop on your left foot, and move your right foot to position 4, off the ground.

Seventh beat: Hop on your left foot, and tap the ball of your right foot at position 4.

Eighth beat: Hop on your left foot, and begin exercise again.

What this exercise amounts to is hopping on your left foot on

52

every beat of the drum, and tapping your right foot on every other beat of the drum. Try switching the entire exercise, hopping on your right foot and tapping your left.

After you have mastered the variations independently of each other, try combining them. Start with simple hop-turns, moving in a circle to your left.

As you turn, combine the cross-over steps, tapping the free foot on alternate beats of the drum. Practice these turns to both left and right, making sure to change from one foot to the other gracefully. When you feel comfortable doing these variations, try doing the exercises on odd beats. You can also try doing the cross-over steps, moving the tapping foot directly from position 1 to position 3, reversing the process.

Side-to-Side Dancing

Using the fast tap-step, you can perform seemingly intricate footwork by moving side to side, crossing one foot over the other as you dance. Try this combination:

Begin by dancing the fast tap-step in place. Now dance to your right with your right foot. Cross the left foot behind the right. Step out to right with your right foot again, and again dance in place for two beats. Step to your left, crossing your right foot behind your left. Step out to your left with your left foot, and finish dancing in place. You can also do this exercise crossing your feet in front of each other.

Drag Step

An interesting variation of the hop-turn is the drag step. As you hop in a circle to your left on your left foot, drag your right foot in position 3, as shown in the accompanying photo.

Body Positions

Two variations of fancy dancing, not ordinarily used in slow war-dancing, are shown in accompanying photos:

The dancer executes the drag step.

Dancer's arms are bent at elbows with knuckles parallel.

Typical fancy-dance body position.

Hop turns — dancers' arms bent at elbow, knuckles parallel. Leaning far to one side.

This then is fancy dancing. After you have become proficient in the exercises described in this chapter, you are ready to learn the routines of some of the popular American Indian dances. Remember, there is no limit to the variations of fancy dancing that you can create. It is a style of dancing in which each dancer has a chance to show off a variety of steps and body movements all of his own design.

Once I saw an Oto Indian win a war-dance contest in Oklahoma by turning a flip in mid air. He took quite a chance: if he had landed off-beat, he would have been automatically disqualified. Although "tricks" should be discouraged, this event shows you that just about anything goes in fancy dancing.

IX

The War-Dance

An old Sioux told me how the Indians of his tribe danced the war-dance before they were put on reservations.

When a war party returned from a raid on the enemy, all the people gathered in the council lodge to watch the men dance their brave deeds. Each warrior got up and told the people about the battle by showing his deeds in pantomime. One by one the warriors danced around the lodge, gesturing in sign language, creeping, stalking the enemy, looking for trail signs, and finally finding the foe, killing him, and taking his scalp.

A chorus of singers accompanied the pantomime — not with an actual song, but rather a pulsating "hi yu ho" as they beat on a hollowed log with sticks. As each dancer finished recounting his deeds, he received "haus" of applause from the spectators. The war dances or, more rightly, story dances, lasted far into the night, ending only when the last dancer had told about his prowess as a warrior.

Today, although there are no war deeds to portray, the Indians still enjoy the so-called war-dance. But today, it is a social dance in which young and old don their feathers and bells and dance to the throbbing drum and pulsating voices of singers. It is a dance in which each dancer can show off his ability to dance in the traditional manner of his forefathers, keeping careful time to drum and song, still enjoying the applause of the spectators.

The war-dance is the most popular dance of the American Indian. Both men and women join in the dancing. Indian singers pride themselves in the number of war-dance songs they can sing.

Before discussing how to perform the dance, it's appropriate

56

to mention some of its history. Contrary to popular opinion, the dance — as it is performed today — was done by the warriors after returning from the warpath, not before leaving. The war-dance was really a part of a *victory* celebration.

The term *war-dance* itself is misleading nowadays. Indians and hobbyists use the term to designate a free-style method of dancing in which there is no set routine. In the war-dance, individuals perform dance steps independent of each other, yet as a group.

War-dance, translated into Indian languages, changes with tribe and region. For example, the Sioux of North Dakota, and the Blackfeet and Blood of Montana, call it grass dance. This name refers to the old-time Indian custom of wearing braided grass in their belts to simulate scalps. The Sioux of South Dakota learned this dance from the Omaha Indians who performed it the same way as the Montana tribes. The South Dakota Sioux called the dance Omaha dance, naming it for the tribe from whom they learned it.

Among the Shoshone and Arapaho of Wyoming, the dance is called wolf dance (warriors, and especially scouts, were sometimes referred to as wolves), and the Chippewa of Minnesota and Wisconsin call it powwow dance (a term more popular among non-Indians than among Indians).

In Oklahoma, where native Indian languages have given way to English, the traditional war-dance of the Omaha, Ponca, Oto, Osage, and Pawnee is called the straight dance, because of the easy-flowing, unpretentious way these tribes dance it. The modern form of the war-dance in Oklahoma is called the fancy or fast war-dance, or just war-dance. The straight dance is easily distinguished from the war dance in Oklahoma by the costumes the dancers wear. In straight dancing there is an obvious absence of fancy featherwork. On the other hand, featherwork is the mainstay of the fancy war-dance costume. The best performers of the fancy war-dance are the Comanche, Kiowa, Cheyenne and Arapaho.

Although the war-dance goes by many names, members of all

tribes can easily dance it together at "Pan-Indian" gatherings, because the songs are similar.

Drumming and Songs

War-dance drumming is the steady, one-quarter time described in Chapter 3. The dance is performed in three tempos — slow, medium, and fast. The slow and medium dances are sometimes called old-style or old-time dances. The fast tempos are used for the fancy war-dance and dance contests.

War-dance songs are similar among all tribes, even though the costumes and dancing style vary. And war-dance songs of all tribes have the same ending. It takes seven beats to sing it, and it is sung on one note. Dancers listen for this ending, which enables them to stop dancing on precisely the last beat of the drum. This is particularly important in the contest dances; dancers are disqualified if their bells keep ringing after the drum has stopped.

A number of war-dance songs have been recorded and may be bought from the suppliers listed in Chapter 22. It is a good idea to listen to these songs over and over to get the feel of Indian music and drumming. Learning the songs will make you a better dancer. War-dance songs are particularly easy to learn; most of them contain no words. The singers simply use syllables such as "ya," "we," "he," and "yo" to carry the tune of the song. As each song ends, you will hear these syllables (with slight variation depending on the tribe):

we yo he ye he ye yo!

Notice there are seven syllables. The drum is beaten progressively louder on the last five beats, ending on a very loud beat.

A war-dance song is sung over from six to eight times, sometimes more, to form a complete war-dance. Recorded songs are short so that a number of songs can be placed on one side of the record, but live war-dances last as long as ten or fifteen minutes. Familiarize yourself with war-dance songs by playing the records over and over, or by recording a record on tape several times over, and playing the tape through.

You'll notice that most war-dance songs begin on a very high note and gradually work down to a lower vocal register. As the songs become lower, it is an indication that the song is about to end.

While listening to these songs, practice the war-dance steps to them. You will notice that in the middle of each war-dance song, there is a series of accented beats. In Oklahoma songs, there are usually three beats; in other war-dance songs, there are five to seven beats. These accented beats keep you in time with the drum and song. On the loud beats, the tap of the tap-step (or toe of the toe-heel) is performed.

The Dance

Before the song begins, all dancers sit or stand around the perimeter of the dance area. As the singers start the song, a few dancers rise and begin dancing the tap-step, or fast tap-step, moving toward the center of the dance area. Soon all dancers rise and begin dancing *counterclockwise* around the dance area (see description of dance area in Chapter 20). In Oklahoma the dancers usually dance clockwise.

Each dancer performs his own combination of slow or fast war-dance steps and variations. The dancers may dance to the side, or in place, or sometimes even backwards for a few steps, but the general direction of the dancers is around the center of the area. Friends usually dance together side by side, and may talk and joke with each other while dancing. At times they separate, do a few fancy variations, and then team up again to join the rest of the dancers in the counterclockwise movement.

Women perform the tap-step, or toe-heel, moving *clockwise* around the men on the perimeter of the dance area. I have seen the women of some woodland tribes, however, dance right next to the drum in the center of the area. Women dance with little variation in steps and few changes in body movement. Their bodies are held erect, and their hands kept to the side or on their hips. They always wear long, fringed shawls over their shoulders or carry them folded neatly over one arm. As they dance, the fringe sways gently in time with their movements.

The war-dance lasts for six to eight renditions of the song. At the beginning of each rendition, the song gets louder, and the dancers dance furiously, using all of their best steps. All dancers stop on the last beat of the drum.

The Tail

Every war-dance officially ends with a tail, or encore. This is a short rendition of the song which begins a split-second after the main dance ends. Everybody dances and stops on the last beat of the tail song. The Sioux, Blackfeet, and Cree sometimes sing two tails, or — if the dancers seem to be over-enthusiastic dancing — the singers will begin the war-dance songs all over again.

During the tail, the men continue dancing counterclockwise, but the women dance *in place,* facing the center of the area. Some women simply bob up and down in time to the song during the tail.

Head and Tail Dancers

At Oklahoma powwows, one dancer of exceptional ability is selected as the *head* dancer. It is his duty to lead every dance, and no one else may begin until he has started. Some tribes also select a man to dance alone during the tail. In olden times, the tail dancer was chosen from among those who were particularly brave in battle. In was considered a great honor to be tail dancer.

The War-Dance Contest

The war-dance is the best dance in which to judge a dancer's ability. In the war-dance contest, the counterclockwise movement and the tail are eliminated. The contestants spread out on the dance area so that the judges may easily watch them. During the contest, each one dances within a two- or three-foot circle.

Ideally, there is one judge for every three contestants. The singers sing the first song, during which each judge selects the best one of his three dancers. The two of each group who are eliminated, retire from the dance area, leaving the best dancers. The finalists dance, and the judges vote among themselves to choose first, second, and third place. Those eliminated leave the dance

60

Ronnie Theisz, member of the Medicine Drum Dancers of New York City, competing at the First Annual New Jersey Indian Homecoming Powwow. He is wearing a typical Winnebago-style costume. (Photo: courtesy of Powwow Trails.)

area, and the three winners remain to dance a short dance for the spectators. They then receive cash prizes, ribbons, or articles of handicraft.

The contests are usually separated into junior and senior divisions. Any number of contestants may enter. Juniors and seniors may again be divided into old-time dancers and fancy dancers. There are also contests for children one to eight, and buckskin-dress or cloth-dress contests for women and girls.

Most judges base their evaluations on the contestants' style of dancing, but there are some standards against which dancers are judged. One is the dancer's ability to keep perfect time with the drum and song, and to end on the last beat of the drum. If a dancer loses any article of costuming during the contest, he is automatically disqualified.

Costumes and War-Dances and Contests

The costumes described in Chapter 19 are appropriate for the war-dances. The general rule is that the Oklahoma fancy-dance costume, the Mesquakie costume, and the northern-style outfit are worn for the fancy war-dance. All other costumes are worn in the old-style war-dances. The straight-dance costume is reserved for the straight dance. At Indian celebrations, an appropriate costume is most important. Tradition is important to an Indian, and he would feel insulted to see a dancer dressed improperly.

More and more hobbyists are recognizing the importance of correct costuming. At many contests, dancers are judged on their ability to dance in the manner of the tribe that their costume represents.

Here are some other general rules. If you dress like an old-timer, limit your steps to the tap-step, toe-heel, and simple variations. Good head movement is important. If you wear a straight-dance costume, do the tap-step or fast tap-step, but with little variation. The straight dance is an easy-flowing style of dancing. When wearing the fancy Oklahoma, Mesquakie, or northern-style costume, use all the fancy war-dance variations you know.

Although the routine of the war-dance described in this chapter seems elementary, it is up to the individual to make the dance exciting. I have seen Indians and hobbyists dance from dawn to dusk, performing one war-dance after the other, resting only a few minutes between dances. It's the kind of dance that grows on you. For the Indian, the war-dance provides an opportunity to dress up in the traditional costume of his forefathers, and relive the past, even if only for the duration of a song.

62

X

The Round Dance

If the war-dance is first in popularity among the American Indian, surely the round dance and its variations rank second.

Virtually every tribe in the United States performs the round dance in one form or another. It is purely a social dance in which men and women participate. Possibly this accounts for its prominence. It is one of the few dances in which men and women take part on equal terms. In the war-dance, the women stay around the outside rim of the dance area, but in the round dance, they literally dance shoulder to shoulder with the menfolk.

The round dance, one of the oldest of Indian dances, may well have originated as a woman's dance. Some tribes speak of a scalp dance in which women shuffled about in a circle, carrying the war trophies of their male relatives. The round dance among some tribes is still called shuffling-feet dance.

Drumming and Songs

The drum is played in three-quarter time with the second beat omitted (see Chapter 3). The first beat is played louder than the third — LOUD-soft, LOUD-soft. The usual tempo is $\quarternote = 160$. The dance begins and ends on the loud beat.

The most melodious songs are sung in the round dance. Like the war-dance songs, the round-dance songs begin on a very high note and gradually descend to a low register. While some tribes sing the round-dance songs using words, most of the songs are made up of meaningless syllables. All round-dance songs end:

we ya ha ya we ya ha ya yo!

There are many fine recordings of round-dance songs (see Chapter 22).

Round-Dance Step

Men and women perform the same step. Assume the Indian stance with your weight on your right foot. The step takes two beats:

First (LOUD) beat: Step to your left; your weight shifts to your left foot.
Second (soft) beat: Slide your right foot to meet your left. Your weight shifts to your right foot.

Repeat over and over for the entire dance.

Step to your left. Your weight shifts to your left foot.

Slide your right foot to meet your left. Your weight shifts to your right foot.

The Dance

Men and women form a circle facing the center. If there are many dancers, more than one circle may be formed, one inside the other. When there are few dancers, the circle becomes an arc. As the song begins, the dancers dance in a *clockwise* circle, doing the round-dance step.

There is no order in which the men and women stand. But among some tribes, a woman may ask a man to dance next to her. Most dancers dance with their hands at their sides, but some tribes hold hands and swing them back and forth in time to the drum.

The Forty-Nine

One of the most popular dances for teen-agers and young adults is the forty-nine. Although practically all tribes dance some version of it, the dance described here was learned in Oklahoma. While the forty-nine is very popular among Indian people, hobbyists rarely perform the dance, because the songs are difficult to sing.

It is impossible to determine just how the forty-nine got its name. It is a recent dance, probably dating back to the turn of the century, but the songs are very old. Some Indians say that the dance was named after a battle in which fifty warriors set out against the enemy, but only one returned. The dance, so the story goes, was performed in honor of the forty-nine slain. I have heard another version: forty-nine warriors returned, and only one was slain. The most recent theory states that the name of the dance is somehow connected with the gold-rush days of 1849, and that a group of Oklahoma Indians took the name from a county fair side-show which had a gold-rush theme.

Drumming and Songs

Like the round dance, the forty-nine is played in three-quarter time with the second beat omitted. The first beat is played louder than the third. The forty-nine's tempo, however, is much faster — $\downarrow = 200$ — and sometimes resembles the fast war-dance tempo.

Only the best Oklahoma singers know the beginnings of the forty-nine songs; they are difficult to sing. Everybody, however, knows the choruses and sings right along with the singers at the drum. The endings of the songs are the same as those of round-dance songs.

The Forty-Nine Step

The step resembles walking sideways to your left, taking a step on each alternating (LOUD) beat of the drum. Begin with your weight on your right foot.

First (LOUD) beat: Step to your left on your left foot. You lean slightly to your left, and your weight shifts to your left foot.
Second (soft) beat: (No step is taken.)
Third (LOUD) beat: Move your right foot near to your left (about two inches apart). You shift your weight to your right foot, and you are ready to step with your left foot again.
Fourth (soft) beat: (No step is taken.)

The forty-nine. Dancers lock arms and step clockwise around the circle.

66

The Dance

The singers take their places in the center of the dance area and begin the forty-nine songs, dancing the forty-nine step clockwise as they sing. A few dancers immediately form a tight circle around the singers, lock arms, and begin dancing the forty-nine step clockwise. More dancers form another circle around the first one. Finally there are many concentric circles of dancers around the singers. Each circle moves slowly clockwise, stepping on alternating beats of the drum. The singers sing one song after another.

In Oklahoma, the dancers try to get into the circle closest to the singers so that they may hear the songs more clearly. The circles of dancers are always changing as some dancers leave and newcomers join. There is constant movement within the circles.

Each time the familiar chorus of the song is sung, all the dancers join in with the singers. Many of the forty-nine songs have words. One goes:

She got mad at me because I said hello to my old-timer.

Once a forty-nine gets started, it is danced all night.

Costume

The forty-nine is not a dance for spectators. The Indians dance it for their own enjoyment. While the round dance is performed in costume or street clothes, the forty-nine is always danced in street clothes. The forty-nine is an excellent dance after the wardances are over. Dancers may change into more comfortable clothing and return to the dance area for hours of more dancing in the forty-nine.

XI

The Two-Step

The two-step, or — as it is sometimes called — the rabbit dance, shares popularity with the round dance and forty-nine. It is danced by nearly all tribes, but is especially popular in North and South Dakota and Oklahoma. It is one of the few Indian dances in which men and women dance together as partners.

Apparently influenced by the Whiteman, the two-step was popular among the Cree Indians of Canada and Montana. From them, the Sioux learned it, and soon it was being danced by all tribes of the northern and southern plains. Today the dance is popular wherever Indians and hobbyists gather to dance. The name *rabbit dance* comes from the Sioux who call the Cree (from whom they learned the dance) rabbit-skin wearers. The Oklahoma Indians call it two-step.

Drumming and Songs

The drum is played in three-quarter time, but slightly slower than in the round dance. The first beat is played louder than the third: LOUD-soft, LOUD-soft. The usual tempo is ♩ = 136. The dance begins and ends on the loud beat.

The songs sung on the North and South Dakota reservations contain words and mainly are love songs "set to the drum." Many old love songs are sung to rabbit dances. In rabbit songs that contain words, the first chorus is sung without words, and the second chorus with words. Many of the old love songs, which young bucks sang to their sweethearts from the safety of the darkness, are now made into rabbit songs. They usually evoke the laughter of the old-timers. Here is the translation of one song:

> *Dearie* (this English word is used to begin many Sioux rabbit songs)
> *I loved you most, but now you're going away.*
> *You'll be gone so long . . .*
> *Take my hand for the last time.*

And another says:

> *Dearie, now you're going home.*
> *Don't be sad.*
> *Later on, I'll remember you.*

The endings of the rabbit songs are the same as those of the round dances and forty-nines.

The Two-step Step

The two-step takes six beats to perform. Assume the Indian stance, your weight on your right foot.

First (LOUD) beat: Step forward on your left foot. Both feet are parallel, and the toes of your right foot are even with the arch of your left.

Second (soft) beat: Step forward on your right foot. Again both feet are parallel. Your right foot is slightly in front of your left.

Third (LOUD) beat: Step forward on your left foot.

Fourth (soft) beat: Step forward on your right foot.

Fifth (LOUD) beat: Step *back* on your left foot. Both feet are parallel. Your right foot is slightly in front of your left.

Sixth (soft) beat: Step back on your right foot and you are ready to begin again.

Repeat the step over and over for the entire dance.

The Dance

Men and women form partners holding each other.

The man is always on the left of the woman. The direction of the dance is clockwise around the outer perimeter of the dance

Men and women form couples. Here they step forward on their left foot on the first beat of the drum.

In the red-and-white dance the partners face each other as in a waltz.

Step back on your left foot. The way the dancers hold each other resembles the ice-skater's position.

Another view of the red-and-white dance position.

area. Usually there is one lead couple who takes the floor as soon as the song begins. The rest of the couples queue in behind them.

The dance lasts for about six to eight songs. At the end of the first "set," the singers and dancers stop. Immediately they begin again for another six to eight songs. At the conclusion, the singers sing a short tail, and the dancers turn around and dance counter-clockwise (the man is now on the inside of the circle).

Costumes

Because this dance is sometimes interspersed between war-dances, the dancers wear war-dance costumes. However, the dance may also be danced in street clothes. Usually the women ask the men to dance. A woman is expected to wear or carry a shawl.

The Red-and-White Dance

This dance, although no longer performed, was once a popular dance of the Sioux. It is really a variation of the rabbit dance. It is called red and white because, although the songs and steps are Indian, the pattern in which they were danced was influenced by the waltz or fox trot. Red-and-white drumming and singing are the same as in the two-step. In the red-and-white dance, however, the dancers face each other as in the waltz. And instead of performing the rabbit-dance step forward and backward, they do it to the side and in no particular direction. There is no file of dancers. They simply spread out on the dance floor as in any kind of ballroom dancing.

XII

The Scout Dance

The scout dance — which the Sioux sometimes called the sneak-up dance — tells the story of scouts on the warpath. The dancers portray the actions of warriors looking for their enemies. This is an old dance of the Sioux, dating back to the time when small war parties traveled hundreds of miles to meet their enemies, the Shoshone and Crow. The sneak-up dance is still performed today as a show dance at many of the Sioux celebrations in South Dakota.

Drumming and Song

The song is divided into two distinct parts. In the first part, the drum thunders; in the second part, the drum is played in medium one-quarter time ($\downarrow$=180). This song has been recorded on Canyon records (No. ARP 167-a). After you have learned the dance, practice it to the record.

The scout-dance song tells about a war leader who was wounded in the thick of battle. Here are the words:

Le yuha manipe
Eca blokaunta ca wašošeyape lo.
Le yuha manipe.

Translation:

They are carrying him (for he is wounded).
Behold the hero, for he was in the thick of battle.
They are carrying him.

The Dance

Any number of dancers may perform. They begin by forming a line facing the audience. Dancers are about four feet apart.

During the first part of the dance, the drum thunders, and the dancers kneel on one knee, or squat, and pretend to be looking for enemies. While shaking one leg rapidly in time with the thunder drumming, they shade their eyes, point to imaginary tracks on the ground, and listen for hoofbeats of enemy horses. Some check the direction of the wind by throwing dust in the air, while others test their weapons.

During the second part of the dance, the drum and song change to a medium war-dance beat. The dancers arise and dance toward the audience, using fast tap-steps and variations. They stop on the last beat of the drum.

During the beginning of the scout dance, the dancers squat low and imitate the actions of scouts on the warpath.

73

Immediately, the drum begins to thunder again. The dancers walk back to their original line, and again begin acting out the role of the scout. Again the drum changes to a medium war-dance beat, and the dancers rise and dance forward. This sequence is performed four times. The last war-dance is slightly faster than the preceding three, and the dancers spread out on the dance area, dancing fast and furiously, using all of their best fancy-dance steps. Suddenly the drum stops. It begins again as the dancers perform a quick tail.

Costumes

Old-time Sioux costumes are ideal for the sneak-up dance, but other dance costumes may be worn.

The Ruffle Dance

The ruffle dance is performed by the tribes in Oklahoma as a dance contest. It is mentioned here because the pattern of the dance resembles that of the scout dance.

Drumming and Song

As in the scout dance, the song is divided into two parts. In the first part, the drum thunders. The second part is a very fast one-quarter time ($\quarternote = 320$). A good recording of the ruffle dance can be found on American Indian Soundchiefs.

The Dance

Any number of dancers may participate. They form a line facing the audience and spaced approximately four to five feet apart. As the thunder-drumming begins, each dancer shakes the bells on one leg very rapidly, his free leg trembling to keep in time with the drum. All of a sudden, the drumming changes to a very fast war-dance. The dancers then begin performing their best fancy-dance steps in place. They stop sharply with the last beat of the drum. The entire sequence is done four times.

Costume

The fancy feathered costume of the Oklahoma Indians is preferred in this dance.

74

XIII

The Flag Dance

The American Indian is very patriotic. During both world wars and the Korean conflict, Indians were among the first to volunteer for active duty, and many were cited for exceptional bravery in combat.

During peacetime, the Indian's patriotism is evident in the way he shows respect for the American flag. All Indian celebrations begin with veterans raising the Stars and Stripes while the singers sing the flag song — the Indian counterpart of the national anthem. When the flag song is sung, the people rise.

Depending on the tribe, there are various ways in which the flag dance is done. Here are two variations popular in South Dakota and Oklahoma.

The Sioux Flag Dance

I first witnessed the Sioux flag dance at the opening ceremony of the 1951 Fourth of July Celebrations on the Pine Ridge Reservation in South Dakota. At one time, this dance was very popular, but has given way to a newer opening ceremony. This is the way it was originally performed:

Drumming and Songs

The drum is played in a three-quarter beat at $\quarternote = 160$. Although the Sioux used a special song, any round-dance song may be used.

The Flag-Dance Step

First (LOUD) beat: Step forward on your left foot. The arch of your left foot is even with the toes of your right.

Second (SOFT) beat: Step forward on your right foot. Both feet are parallel, the left slightly ahead of the right.

Repeat this over and over for the entire dance (it resembles the two-step, with the backward movement eliminated).

The Dance

Any number of dancers may dance. Two men who have served in the armed services are selected to carry an American flag. They hold it between them by the upper corners (a flagpole is never used). The rest of the dancers file in behind them in couples. Two men, two women, or a man and woman may dance together, but do not hold each other as in the two-step. Their arms are held at their sides or on their hips.

The drumming and singing begins, and the lead dancers dance clockwise around the perimeter of the dance area swinging the flag forward and backward in time to the drum. The other couples join in behind them. As the dancers pass by, the spectators rise, the men removing their hats. The dancers perform one revolution around the dance area, and the dance is over. The two veterans then attach the flag to a pole in the center of the dance area and raise the flag. This officially opens the dance.

Nowadays the Sioux open their celebrations with another kind of national anthem, which is sung to a slow beating of the drum. There is no dance, but everyone rises while two veterans raise the flag. An honor guard of veterans in military uniforms stand by with loaded rifles. As the flag is attached to the rope, the commander of the honor guard gives the command, and the riflemen fire a three-gun salute. As the last shot cracks out, the singers dramatically begin this high-pitched flag song:

Tunkašilayapi tawapaha kin oihanke šni najin yelo.
Iyohlate oyate kin wicicagin kta ca lecamon.

Translation:

The flag of the United States will fly forever.
Beneath it, the Indian people will grow.

When the flag reaches the top of the pole, all veterans perform the war-dance. There is a special song sung for this dance, which is repeated in the afternoon when the flag is lowered. The words express the Indian's loyalty.

76

Le yuha manipe.
Tunkašilayapi tawapaha ca he yuha manipe
Lakota hokšila he ohitika can he yuha manipe
Tunkašilayapi tawapaha ca he yuha manipe.

Translation:

They are carrying it.

They are carrying the flag of the United States.

The brave Indian boys (Indian soldiers) are carrying it.

They are carrying the flag of the United States.

The words are said to refer to the Indian boys who carried the United States flag into battle during the wars.

In this impressive ceremony, the modern, patriotic American Indian stands shoulder to shoulder with the old people of the tribe, and both show respect — each in his own way — to the country they love.

The Oklahoma Processional

Among the Oklahoma Indians, the processional opens each dance. It may be danced to a round dance as the Sioux flag dance, or it may be danced as a slow war-dance. Either way, veterans lead the dance, carrying a flag on a pole. They are followed by the Gold Star mothers, and then by the rest of the dancers. The direction of the dance is clockwise around the perimeter of the dance area. The step is either the step described for the Sioux flag dance, or the slow tap-step. Practically each tribe in Oklahoma has its own flag song, and many of these songs are recorded.

In some of the larger shows, the processional is performed without flags as a show opener. The dancers enter the dance area in two single columns, one column dancing around the perimeter of the dance area clockwise, the other, counterclockwise. When they meet in the center, they end the processional and immediately begin a fast war-dance, or round dance.

XIV

The Shield Dance

The shield dance is a specialty dance of the Oklahoma Indians and a favorite at the American Indian Exposition. It is a story dance in which two dancers "fight" each other. Each dancer carries a spear and shield. During the dance, the dancers feint at each other, raising their spears ominously, and quickly throw up their shields as if to ward off enemy blows.

The shield dance is a perfect show dance. At Anadarko, Oklahoma, many partners dance it simultaneously. The dance can lend a lot of excitement to a show.

Drumming and Song

The dance begins with thunder-drumming that lasts about 45 seconds. For the rest of the dance, the drum is played in medium to fast one-quarter time. While the Indians use a special song, any war-dance song will suffice.

The Shield-Dance Step

The fast tap-step and variations are used throughout the dance.

The Dance

The dancers take their positions at "A" and "B" (see accompanying illustration). The drum begins thundering, and they crouch low, looking at each other cautiously, shaking one leg quickly in time with the drum. They carry lances in their right hands and shields over their left forearms. The dancers peer over their shields at their opponents and shake their lances threateningly.

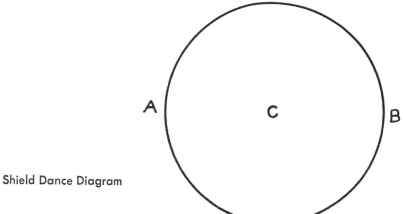

Shield Dance Diagram

Boy Scouts performing the shield dance at the forty-eighth Anniversary Conference of the Order of the Arrow, at the University of Illinois.

The Arrow, an honor camping fraternity of the Boy Scouts of America, employs Indian lore as its theme. It has over 200,000 members. (Photo: courtesy of Boy Scouts of America.)

The dancers peer over their shields and shake their lances threateningly. (Dancer practicing without props.)

The drum changes to a medium one-quarter tempo. The dancers rise and begin dancing the fast tap-step counterclockwise around the circle, keeping their eyes fixed on each other. Their spears are poised, and their shields are held in front of their bodies. The dancers dance half-way around the circle until each occupies the other's original position. They dance in this position for approximately forty-eight beats of the drum.

Now the dancers begin dancing toward each other, crouching low, and then straightening up, stepping from side to side as if they were in the thick of an attack on an enemy. As they approach position "C" they quickly pass each other, never taking their eyes off each other, and dance backward to their original positions. The dancers now dance in place. From the time the dancers start dancing toward each other, this section of the dance takes approximately ninety-six beats.

Suddenly from their own positions, the dancers charge at each other, meeting at position "C". Here they circle around each other, backing off, then closing in. They dance backward half-way back to their original positions, and then charge quickly, touching their lances against each other's shields on the last beat of the drum.

Costumes

The feathered fancy-dance costume of Oklahoma is preferred in this dance. But the old-time Sioux, the northern-style, and the Mesquakie costumes may also be used.

The Shield

The shield may be fashioned from heavy cardboard eighteen inches in diameter and covered with buckskin or lightweight canvas. Paint designs in the center of the shield, and hang feathers from the edge.

The Spear

This is a dance spear and should have no point. You can make one from a three-quarter-inch sapling, or dowel rod, six feet long. It may be decorated with fur and feathers.

XV

The Snake Dance

The snake dance of Oklahoma — sometimes called the Teguia — is a social dance in which the dancers imitate the movements of a snake. The column of dancers represents the snake's head, body, and tail. After the snake dance, the dancers spread out and perform the buffalo dance, which is described in Chapter 16.

Drumming and Song

The drum thunders for a few seconds while the dancers form a line. It then breaks into a medium one-quarter beat. The song is recorded on American Indian Soundchiefs, Kiowa 306, the Kiowa version of the song recorded by White Fox.

The Snake-Dance Step

The snake-dance step is basically a trot in which your left foot remains slightly in front of your right. There is also a rise and fall of your body as you trot, and a synchronized movement of your arms and feet.

Practice the following exercise slowly first. Assume the Indian stance, with your arms held in front of your body, knuckles parallel. Your weight is on your right foot.

First beat: Step forward on your left foot. The toes of your right

The snake dance. Notice arms and hands in above photo. On the first beat drop your left hand to waist level and raise your right hand to chest level. On the second beat reverse the hands, the right dropping to waist level, and the left moving to chest level. This is repeated over and over in time with the foot movements. The hands are held in loose fists.

foot are even with the arch of your left. Both legs are straight. Second beat: Step forward on your right foot. Your left foot is still in front of your right. On this movement, bend your right leg slightly, and lift your left foot off the ground about four inches.

Hold your hands in loose fists in front of your body, as the accompanying photo shows. On the first beat, drop your left hand to waist level, and raise your right hand to chest level. On the second beat, return your hands to the first position. Repeat this over and over in time with the foot movements.

The Dance

Any number of men and women may participate in the snake dance. One man is chosen as the head, or leader of the dance. Another becomes the tail. These positions are always filled by men.

As the drum thunders, the leader enters the dance area, and the rest of the dancers file in behind him, the women interspersed between the men. The tail dancer waits until the column has formed; then he joins, on the end of the line.

The drum changes to the one-quarter beat, and the dancers begin dancing the snake-dance step, following the leader in the spiraling movements of a snake. Soon the leader holds up his right hand and yells. The dancers immediately turn around and begin following the tail dancer who likewise leads them snake-fashion around the dance area. Each time the head or tail of the snake wants to reverse the direction of the column, he simply holds up his hand and yells. This happens many times during the dance. When the dance has ended, the dancers spread out on the dance area and get ready for the buffalo dance.

Costumes

Since this dance is danced primarily in Oklahoma, most of the dancers wear the fancy-dance costumes. Any costume, however, may be worn.

XVI

The Buffalo Dance

Old Indians speak of the buffalo with great respect. It was the main source of life for the plains Indian, and he believed that the buffalo was a messenger of the great Spirit sent down to the earth people to provide all of their necessities. How true it was. The great shaggy beasts provided not only meat and soup, warm robes and moccasins, parfleche and tipis — there were hundreds of additional uses of the buffalo.

The buffalo provided marrow for treating wounds or for making paint, horns for musical instruments or cooking ladles, and ribs for children to use as sleds. Buffalo hair was used to stuff dolls. The animal's stomach was cleaned and used as a cooking pot. The sinew was used for sewing. No part of the buffalo was wasted.

Because the buffalo played such an important part in the everyday life of the Indian, there were many songs and dances performed in honor of the buffalo. Every tribe had some form of tribute.

Sometimes dances were performed before leaving on a buffalo hunt, to invoke the power of the great beast. In these dances, the hunters wore the shaggy buffaloskin robes and buffalo horns as a costume and imitated the animal's movements. They carried the bows and arrows, the lances, and later the guns with which they hunted the buffalo. Although the days of the buffalo hunt are gone, the Indians still dance the buffalo dance. The dance as it is

Black Bear, a Sioux Indian from South Dakota, wearing a buffalo-dance headdress made from the head and horns of a buffalo. Nowadays, Plains Indians dance the buffalo dance in standard war-dance costumes. (Photo: Bell.)

During the thunder-drumming, the dancers move about imitating the actions of buffalo.

described here is performed by the southern-plains tribes of Oklahoma at their Annual Exposition. Traditionally, it follows the snake dance.

Drumming and Song

Both thunder-drumming and a steady beat are used in the buffalo dance. The steady beat is the one-quarter beat played half-time at $\quarternote = 60$. A recording of the buffalo-dance song can be found on American Indian Soundchiefs (*Kiowa Buffalo Dance*, sung by White Fox). Although the song is labeled Kiowa, the Comanche claim to be the rightful owners and originators of the dance.

The Buffalo-Dance Steps

There are two movements in the buffalo dance that correspond with the thunder-drumming and the one-quarter beat.

During the one-quarter beat, the dancers stand in place and perform the jump step.

During the thunder-drumming, the dancers scatter over the dance area, each one going in his own direction, moving his head from side to side as if he were a buffalo milling about on the prairie. Sometimes, the dancers brush up against each other slightly, imitating the movements of the buffalo.

During the one-quarter beat, the dancers stand in place and perform the following jump step:

Assume the Indian stance, but bend both knees slightly. On each beat of the drum, jump, so that both feet come down on each beat of the drum. Your hands are on your hips. The action should be absorbed from the waist down, so that your head "stays in place" as you jump. These jumps are done in place or in a small semicircle, as you move to your right and then to your left. You may also take a few steps forward between jump steps, bending your head low.

The Dance

The buffalo dance begins at the conclusion of the snake dance. The dancers take their place on the dance area, scattering in every direction.

The drum thunders, and the dancers walk about, imitating the movement of the buffalo, bending their heads low, or moving them from side to side. This lasts for about forty-five seconds.

The drum changes to the steady one-quarter time, and the dancers perform the jump step in place, dancing in small semicircles for fourteen beats.

The drum thunders again, and the dancers begin walking about.

Again the drum changes to the one-quarter time, and the dancers perform the jump step for twenty-eight beats.

The entire sequence is then repeated again.

Costumes

Although some of the southwestern tribes dance their version of the buffalo dance in horned bonnets and buffalo-skin leggings, the Oklahoma tribes use traditional war-dance costumes.

XVII

The Stomp Dance

After the spectators have left the grandstand at the American Indian Exposition in Anadarko, Oklahoma, the young Indian people change from their costumes into their street clothes and return to the dance area for the stomp dance.

This is a dance that originated among the Creek and Seminole of Georgia and Florida, but it is currently danced by nearly all the younger generation of Oklahoma Indians.

Drumming and Songs

There is no drumming in the stomp dance. Instead, some women wear turtle-shell and tin-can rattles around their legs. This provides the accompaniment for the song. Those who wear the rattles are called shakers. It's common to hear one girl ask another, "Are you going to shake tonight?" meaning, is she going to wear her rattles and dance in the stomp dance.

During the stomp dance, many short songs are sung by the dancers. Some of these have been recorded by American Indian Soundchiefs. One version, the *Four-Corners Dance,* is available as Recording #302 by Joe Hicks and his group.

In the stomp dance, the leader sings out a call and the rest of the dancers sing the answer. The best stomp-dance leaders are men who have good voices and know a great variety of stomp-dance calls.

The stomp-dance song begins with a traditional opening call and answer. But, after the introduction, each leader sings his calls in whatever order he chooses.

Stomp-dance leaders have individual styles of dancing. Here the leader waves his right arm back and forth as if he were fanning himself in time to the song.

The Stomp-Dance Step

The men simply trot in time to the rhythm of the song. The shakers, however, perform a more complicated step.

First beat: Tap your right heel in front of your body (this resembles the tap-step, except that the heel is tapped instead of the ball of the foot).
Second beat: Step on your right foot.
Third beat: Tap your left heel in front of your body.
Fourth beat: Step on your left foot.

This step, and the men's trot, is performed at ♩=380 which is extremely fast. The heel-tapping of this step causes the rattles to shake, producing the correct rhythm. The step is very strenuous, and only the best women dancers can act as shakers.

The Dance

The dancers form a single line: first the leader, next a shaker, then the second (a man who knows all of the answers to the calls and who can lead the responses), another shaker, and so on. The shakers always dance near the front of the line. Behind them, all the men and women who wish to dance fall in.

As the dance begins, all the dancers walk casually behind the leader. He leads them slowly around the dance area in no particular direction. After all the dancers are in the line, the leader calls out:

    Hee-yu wo-oooooooooooooo.

And the dancers answer:

    Hee-yu wo-oooooooooooooo.

At this point, everyone yelps very loudly.

Again the leader calls out:

    Hee-yu wo-oooooooooooooo.

The dancers respond:

    Hee!

And then, as the dancers still casually walk about the dance area, they shout out the following calls and answers:

SECTION "A"

    Leader: Hee-yu wo-ooooooooo.
    Dancers: Hee!
    Leader: Hee-yu wo-ooooooooo.
    Dancers: Hee!
    Leader: Hah hay!
    Dancers: Hah hay!
    Leader: Hah hay!
    Dancers: Hah hay!
    Leader: Hah hah!
    Dancers: Hah hah!
    Leader: Hah hah!
    Dancers: Hah hah!
    Leader: Hee yay!
    Dancers: Hee yay!
    Leader: Hee yay!
    Dancers: Hee yay!

At this point, the leader stops walking and begins a trot. The rest of the dancers join in, the shakers shaking their rattles vigorously. The calls and the answers now are sung to the rhythm of the rattles ($\downarrow = 380$).

SECTION "B"

Leader: Ay hee yay.
Dancers: Ay hee yay.
Leader: Ay hee yay.
Dancers: Ay hee yay.
Leader: Ay hee yay.
Dancers: Ay hee yay.
Leader: Ay hee yay.
Dancers: Ay hee yay.
Leader: Hoh ee yah.
Dancers: Hoh ee yah.
Leader: Hoh ee yah-ah.
Dancers: Hoh ee yah-ah.
Leader: Hoh ee yay.
Dancers: Hoh ee yay.
Leader: Hoh ee yah-ah.
Dancers: Hoh ee yah-ah.
Leader: Hoh ee yay.
Dancers: Hoh ee yay.
Leader: Hay hay.
Dancers: Hay hay.
Leader: Hee ee yay.
Dancers: Hee ee yay.
Leader: Hee ee yay-ay.
Dancers: Hee ee yay-ay.
Leader: Hee ee yay-ay.
Dancers: Hee ee yay-ay.
Leader: (Raising his right hand) Hee ee yay!
Dancers: Everyone yelps and stops dancing. They remain single file.

SECTION "C"

At this point, the leader begins his favorite calls. Again the dancers begin trotting in time to the shakers. At the end of each call, the leader raises his right hand, and the rest of the dancers yell. The dancers stop with the end of each song, and resume the trotting and shaking with the beginning of each new call. Here are some favorite calls:

Call (leader)   *Responses* (dancers)

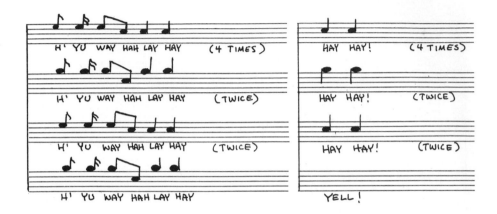

Set 1.

(MUSIC "A-1")   (MUSIC "A-2")
H'yu way hah lay hay.   Hay hay!
(sing four times)   (sing four times)

(MUSIC "B-1")   (MUSIC "B-2")
H'yu way hah lay hay.   Hay hay!
(sing twice)   (sing twice)

(MUSIC "A-1")   (MUSIC "A-2")
H'yu way hah lay hay.   Hay hay!
(sing twice)   (sing twice)

(MUSIC "B-1")
H'yu way hah lay hay.   Yell.

Set 2.
(MUSIC "C-1")
Hee gah yah.
(sing eight times)

(MUSIC "C-2")
Hee yah!
(sing eight times)

(MUSIC "D-1")
Hee gah yah.
(sing twice)

(MUSIC "D-2")
Hee yah!
(sing twice)

(MUSIC "C-1")
Hee gah yah.
(sing twice)

(MUSIC "C-2")
Hee yah!
(sing twice)

(MUSIC "D-1")
Hee gah yah.

Yell.

Set 3.

(MUSIC "E-1")
Way yah kee wo ho.
(sing four times)

(MUSIC "E-2")
Hay ah gah wah.
(sing four times)

(MUSIC "F-1")
Way yah kee way hay.
(sing twice)

(MUSIC "F-2")
Hay yah gah way.
(sing twice)

(MUSIC "E-1")
Way yah kee wo ho.
(sing twice)

(MUSIC "E-2")
Hay yah gah wah.
(sing twice)

(MUSIC "F-1")
Way yah kee way hay.

Yell.

Set 4.

(MUSIC "G-1")
Aw h'yu way h'u way.
(sing twice)

(MUSIC "G-2")
H'yu way h'yu way.
(sing twice)

(MUSIC "H-1")
Au h'yu way h'yu way.

(MUSIC "H-2")
H'yu way h'yu way.

(MUSIC "G-1")
Aw h'yu way h'yu way.

(MUSIC "G-2")
H'yu way h'yu way.

(MUSIC "H-1")
Aw h'yu way h'yu way.

Yell.

Each set of calls and answers may be repeated two or three times. The "yell" comes on the last set only.

Costumes

When performing the stomp dance for spectators, the Creek Indians wear red shirts, ordinary street pants, and western straw

94

SET 4, CALL (LEADER)   RESPONSE (DANCERS)

AW— H'YU WAY H'YU WAY (TWICE)   H'YU WAY H'YU WAY! (TWICE)

AW H'YU WAY H'YU WAY   H'YU WAY H'YU WAY!

AW— H'YU WAY H'YU WAY   H'YU WAY H'YU WAY!

AW H'YU WAY H'YU WAY   YELL!

hats around which red bandanas are tied. Usually, however, the dance is performed in ordinary street clothes. The stomp-dance leader wears a ten-gallon hat.

I have watched the forty-nine and the stomp dances compete for the attention of the dancers at Anadarko. On one side of the dance area, some young bucks decide to start up a forty-nine, beating on a cardboard box, because no drum is available. Soon many circles of dancers form around them, sidestepping to the familiar songs.

Then amidst the din of the forty-nine songs, a stomp-dance leader enters the dance area, followed by his shakers and second. Soon dancers who have been standing around watching join the single file of stomp dancers. The leader begins with "hee yo wo-oooooo" and soon more dancers are running to get in the dance.

If the leader is exceptional, he may draw people away from the forty-nine. If he is mediocre, he may have a difficult time gathering up a following. All night long, the forty-nines and the stomps go on. As new leaders appear in the dance area, more dancers leave the forty-nines and join the stomps, while others who have been waiting eagerly crowd into the openings of the forty-nine circles. This is competition between singers and leaders which continues all night long.

XVIII

The Hoop Dance

One of the most spectacular show dances of all tribes is the hoop dance. The greatest exponents of the dance are the Pueblo Indians of New Mexico. Some authorities believe that the dance was originally performed on the northern plains. Certain tribes there danced with magical hoops through which they sighted enemies. This allegedly gave the dancer control over the souls of his adversaries, so that he could easily kill them on the warpath.

The dance worked its way southward, and in the process, the magic was lost. The southwestern Indians used the hoop dance to demonstrate their agility. The dancers manipulated the hoop around their bodies, stepped in and out of it gracefully, and passed it around and over their bodies without breaking time with the drum.

One hoop led to another. Now it is common to see dancers using two, three, four, or more hoops, moving through them and manipulating them with the ease of a juggler.

In 1961, I watched an Indian dancing with sixteen hoops (I had heard about another who supposedly danced with thirty).

Soon the fancy version of the hoop dance was working its way northward. Although the Pueblos are still considered the best hoop dancers, Indians from all tribes are dancing it across the country.

The hoop dance is really a dance for one person. It is difficult for an audience to concentrate on the exciting tricks if more than one dancer performs at a time.

It is best to learn with one hoop. Tony White Cloud — a world-champion hoop dancer — never used more than four.

The Hoop

Commercial plastic hoops are available from a number of Indian suppliers. Wooden barrel hoops, although not readily available nowadays, make excellent dance hoops. You can also use the inside supports of bass drums, which are available at many music stores. The best hoops, however, and the kind prized by Indians, are made from willow or grapevine.

The diameter of your hoop should be four inches wider than the breadth of your shoulders. If the hoop is any larger, the tricks look too easy.

To make a hoop, simply cut a length of grapevine or willow. Soak it in water for two days, until it is pliable enough to shape into a circle. Overlap the ends about four inches (taper the ends thin so that there is no bulge where the two ends connect). Tie the ends together, preferably with rawhide. At this point, the hoop will be more or less egg-shaped. Soak the hoop in a round washtub. The sides of the washtub act as a mold, and your hoop will be perfectly round after soaking it in the tub overnight.

Most dancers, after the hoop has dried, wrap it with ordinary adhesive tape to allow easy gripping.

The Hoop-Dance Step

The basic step of the hoop dance is the fast tap-step. Some dancers perform the steps double-time, using the trot.

Drumming and Songs

Many Tribes have special songs for the hoop dance, but an ordinary war-dance song may be used. The drum plays a medium to fast one-quarter beat.

The Dance

The hoop dance is a highly individualized dance. Each dancer makes up his own routine. Here are some of the best hoop-dance tricks.

Beginning step. Typically, the dancer begins by dancing into the center of the dance area with the hoop over one shoulder. As he gets to the center, he passes the hoop around his body, from one hand to the other, and holds the hoop over his head, or out in front of his body, as though to show it to the spectators. He then begins to dance in and out of the hoop. He dances in place, or around in small circles. He also may dance in a straight line for eight or ten beats and then change directions.

The most important rule in hoop dancing is to keep the hoop moving all the time. The hoop in constant motion makes the dance appear to be much more difficult than it really is.

In and out of the hoop. Hold the hoop in your right hand.

First beat: Step into the hoop with your right foot.
Second beat: Step into the hoop with your left foot.
Third beat: Step out of the hoop with your right foot.
Fourth beat: Step out of the hoop with your left foot.

Try this same step beginning with your left foot. Also try switching the hoop from your right to left hand on the third beat. Try dancing this step directly forward, and again while dancing in a two-foot circle.

Cross-over. Hold the hoop in your right hand.

First beat: Step into the hoop with your left foot.
Second beat: Step over your left foot with your right foot.
Third beat: Step into the hoop with your left foot.
Fourth beat: Step over your left foot with your right foot.

In this step, only the left foot actually steps into the hoop. The right foot keeps stepping over the left foot, but not into the hoop.

Over the body. Dancing along doing the tap-step, holding the hoop in your right hand, pass it over your head and down over your body. As the hoop reaches your waist level, switch it to your left hand, drop the hoop down past your knees, and step out of it.

Reverse this step, stepping into the hoop with both feet, and then raising the hoop over your head.

98

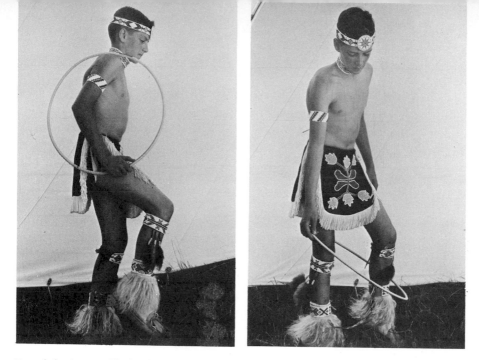

Top, left, Jimmy Clark of Hornell, New York, begins the hoop dance with the hoop placed over one shoulder. At sixteen years old, Jimmy won first place in hoop dancing at the 1964 Monroe Powwow. Top, right, in and out of the hoop. The dancer makes this simple step look tricky by revolving the hoop, switching from right to left hand, as he dances in and out. Bottom, left, the cross-over. This step can be made to look more difficult if the dancer moves in small circles and arcs as he performs it. Bottom, right, over the body. This step may be repeated over and over quickly. Most of the hoop-dance steps are simple. The real skill involved is the dancer's ability to move quickly and gracefully from one step to the next without tangling his feet and breaking rhythm. (Photos: Bettye Lane.)

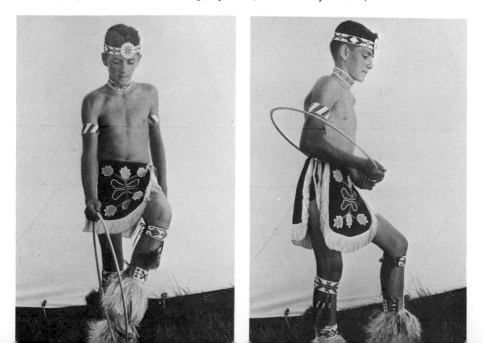

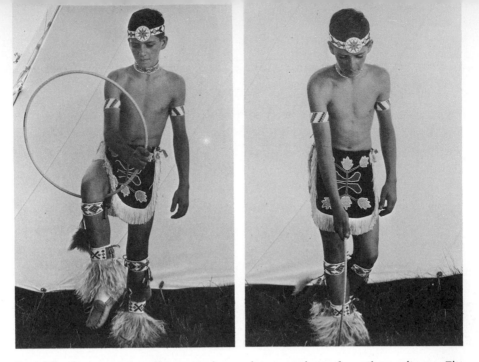

Top, left, the grapevine. This step always draws applause from the audience. The dancer passes the hoop over his head on every other beat of the drum as he simultaneously performs the fast tap-step. Some adroit dancers can manipulate the hoop over their heads on every beat of the drum as they hop in time. Top, right, the criss-cross. This step can be made even more effective by criss-crossing through the hoop and simultaneously turning rapidly in place. Bottom, left, sitting in the hoop. The jumping-rope step described next can also be performed in the sitting position. Bottom, right, jumping rope. This is probably the most difficult trick in the hoop dance. The dancer must gauge himself so that he lands on the beat of the drum. (Photos: Bettye Lane.)

100

Grapevine. Hold the hoop in your right hand, between your legs. Step into the hoop with your right foot, raise your right leg, and let the hoop pass over your head. Now the hoop is in the same position on your left side. Lift your left leg and let the hoop pass over your head. Repeat over and over, quickly.

Criss-cross. Hold the hoop between your legs with your right hand. Step into the hoop with your right foot. Step into the hoop with your left foot crossing over the right. Cross your right foot over your left, keeping both feet in the hoop. Cross your left foot over your right. Repeat over and over. Reverse the process, moving backward. This is effective when done double-time, trotting through the hoop.

Try throwing the hoop out in front of you with a reverse spin. As the hoop rolls back to you, jump up and land with your feet in the criss-cross position in the hoop. This is an effective way to begin the criss-cross step.

Sitting in the hoop. Hold the hoop behind you with both hands and squat down. Let the hoop drop over your head, so that your body is in the hoop. Stand up and dance out of the hoop. Repeat over and over.

Jumping rope. Jump rope through the hoop both frontward and backward without breaking time with the drum. You can also jump rope through the hoop from the sitting-in-the-hoop position.

Picking up the hoop. If you drop the hoop you can pick it up without using your hands. This also makes an effective trick step. Throw the hoop to the ground. Dance around it, stepping lightly in and out of the hoop as it lies on the ground. Then jump into the hoop, and press both feet outward against the sides of the hoop. This will cause the hoop to snap up over your feet. If you press outward with your legs, the hoop will work up your body until you can reach it with your hands.

Optical illusion. Try sitting in the hoop. As the hoop passes over your head stand up quickly and press your arms out the side against the hoop. The hoop will snap up and appear to cut through your body.

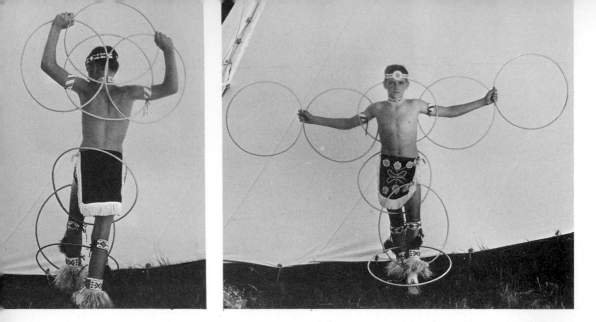

Left, a design formed by interlocking seven hoops. Dancers using more than one hoop begin by throwing all hoops onto the ground and then picking them up one by one without using their hands. Right, a design using eight hoops. The more hoops a dancer uses, the less tricks he can do — he has to concentrate on merely keeping hold of the hoops. Professionals never use more than four hoops. (Photos: Bettye Lane.)

You can make the hoop dance more exciting by using variations of the war-dance steps. Remember to keep the hoop revolving around your body, and constantly in motion.

Designs. Some dancers who use many hoops will form designs with them as they dance. This is the highlight of any dance in which more than four hoops are used.

When you use more than one hoop, make sure that the hoops are cut so that they fit through each other. Most of the steps are the in-and-out-of-the-hoop steps, double grapevines, and passing the hoops over and under the body, one at a time, or simultaneously.

Costumes

Most hoop dancers wear the basic fancy-feather costume of Oklahoma, without the bustles. Indians wear their roaches with the crest feathers removed. It is a good idea to save your roach completely and dance the hoop dance without a headdress.

102

XIX

Costuming

For learning the dances in this book, no special costume is required. Simply wear comfortable, loose clothing and moccasins or sneakers. However, as you develop an interest in American Indian dancing, you may want to join those hobbyists who "build" their own outfits. All that is really needed is one good dance outfit. In this chapter, I'll discuss some of the styles that are popular among Indian and hobbyist dancers.

As you become interested in costume-making, you'll soon learn that — contrary to popular opinion — there is no such thing as a basic Indian costume. This is because over three hundred tribes live in the United States, and each tribe has its own style of craftwork.

Some anthropologists claim that at the time of Columbus, there were over *two thousand* tribes living in North America. That will give you some idea how many styles of costuming existed.

Though it is not my purpose in this chapter to begin to describe the varieties of costumes that exist, I can safely say that most Indian dancers today wear one of about only half a dozen styles of costuming.

To the untrained eye, these costumes may look similar, yet they are quite different in color and design. Some parts, however, are interchangeable.

The Hair Roach

This headdress resembles the roached mane of a horse. The porcupine hair roach is the most highly prized dance headdress. While the warbonnet is worn by old men, the hair roach is the headdress of the young dancer. The roach is made from the guard hair of the porcupine, and deer hair. Some tribes use turkey beard, moose hair, and skunk.

Attached to the inside of the roach is a spreader made of rawhide, silver, or other pliable material, to which is attached the crest — usually one or two feathers that swivel in sockets. Although the hair roach varies in size and shape, it is used with all of the costumes shown here.

Breechcloth, or Aprons

The breechcloth has given way to dance aprons, panels of cloth that hang in front and back from a belt. While aprons are common to all dance outfits; they include a variety of shapes and decorating methods. Notice the variety of design shown in the accompanying photo.

The Bustle

The circular — or sometime U-shaped — arangements of feathers worn on the lower back, and sometimes the neck, have been nicknamed bustles. They derive from a ceremonial piece of costuming known as a crow-belt, and they are especially popular among the fancy war-dancers.

Moccasins

Moccasins are the perfect shoe for the dancer. Some tribes wear soft-sole moccasins, but hard-sole moccasins (usually made of rawhide) are recommended for dancing.

The Indians of North Dakota and Montana, where the grass dance is popular, prefer sneakers to moccasins. Dancers say that it's easier to dance in sneakers and they last longer.

Bells

Bells add rhythm to the drum and song. Originally, Indians used rattles and dew-cloth sashes, for the same effect. When the first traders brought bells, they immediately became popular. Since then, Indians have used bells in practically all dances except

This hair roach is made from yellow porcupine hair. A row of red deer hair is sewn around the outside; skunk hair lines the inside. The crest is made from a rawhide base to which two eagle feathers are attached. (Worn by William Powers.)

This is a Winnebago breechcloth. Notice the fancy ribbonwork and fringe on the front apron. The dancer wears half leggings to match. (Worn by Ronnie Theisz.)

This is a simple Oklahoma breechcloth with ribbonwork and fringe. Most Oklahoma aprons are profusely decorated with beadwork on the front. Some aprons among the Sioux are fully beaded in front. (Worn by William Powers.)

Breechcloth of a northern-style grass-dance costume. Note the full beaded apron in front. (Worn by Ronnie Theisz.) (Photos: Paul Theisz.)

Left, Ronnie Theisz models a Winnebago adaptation of an Oklahoma swing bustle, so called because the horizontal rows of feathers are free to swing back and forth as the dancer moves. Center, the crow belt. This is the piece of costuming from which the back bustle evolved. Shown here is Ronnie Theisz wearing an old-time Sioux costume. Right, Ronnie Theisz wears an Oklahoma straight-dance costume. This costume has a tailored effect and is prized by Oklahoma Indians and hobbyists. (Photos: Paul Theisz.)

ceremonials. It is very difficult for a dancer to dance without them.

Bells come in various sizes and shapes. Indians prefer brass bells, or dull-sounding so-called sheep bells. A *clank* is preferred to a *ring*.

Bells are usually worn around the ankles or under the knees. One or two strands on each leg are ample. In the northern plains, however, the Indians use a great many bells — usually very large ones. These are available through most of the Indian suppliers listed in Chapter 22.

106

Miscellaneous

Though the articles already mentioned are interchangeable among most of the contemporary Indian costumes, there are other parts of costuming that belong to only one style of costuming. By studying the photographs in this chapter, you can see how the different costumes vary. In addition to the hair roach, aprons, bustles, moccasins, and bells, the dancers wear cuffs, armbands, leggings, half-leggings, breastplates, chokers, necklaces, shirts, tights, and miscellaneous other costume parts. These parts and the materials needed to make them are listed in suppliers' catalogs.

It is best to build the outfit of one tribe. By visiting Indian museums, you can learn more about the colors, craft techniques, and designs particular to each tribe.

Most Indian suppliers carry books on how to make Indian costumes. If you have the chance to participate in powwows or visit Indian reservations, it's a good idea to take along a sketchbook, a camera, and plenty of film. Sketch or photograph every interesting costume you see.

Women's costuming. Sioux woman and child wearing traditional beaded buckskin dresses. The yokes of the dresses are solidly beaded. The woman wears a bone hair-pipe necklace. (Photo: Bell.)

Sioux woman wearing beaded buckskin dress and bone hair-pipe necklace. Notice the man's hat decorated with eagle feathers. (Photo: Fiske.)

Women's Costuming

Many women still wear the traditional buckskin dresses, but many are now using cloth dresses made from wool or taffeta.

Streetwear as Costuming

Since most Indians live in the west, their streetwear is western-style clothing, boots, and ten-gallon hats. Dressing for a powwow is like dressing for a square dance. You don't necessarily need a feathered costume. As has been noted in the previous chapters, many of the dances are performed in streetwear. This is especially true on the round dance, forty-nine, stomp dance, two-step, red-and-white dance, and flag dance.

Singers very rarely wear costumes. The typical group around the drum wears ten-gallon hats, Levis, colorful shirts, bandanas, and western-style boots. Some singers may wear feathers in their hats, and beaded hatbands and belts.

Young ladies of the Kunieh Society, a hobbyist group from Indianapolis, Indiana. They are wearing the contemporary costumes of the Winnebago and Potawatomi Indians of Wisconsin and Michigan. Left to right, Margaret Seiler, Carol Puckett, Jane Webb, Karen Kemp, Debbie Hager, Pam Barret. (Photo: courtesy of Powwow Trails.)

XX

The Dance Area

Indian dancing belongs outdoors, with mother earth as the dance floor and the sky as the roof. While a small "council" ring will suffice for some powwows, a more elaborate dance area is required when many dancers perform. No matter how large or small the dance area, there are some things to keep in mind when selecting it.

Choosing the Site

It is important to choose a dance area that is flat, free of stones and roots, and preferably covered with grass mowed to a height of two or three inches. Avoid sandy or muddy areas.

In the days before lawn mowers, Indians simply danced over the selected area until the grass was good and smooth. Today, at the larger celebrations, a water truck stands by to wet down the dance area during intermissions to eliminate some of the dust.

Be sure to fill in all holes. A dancer stumbling into a hole can easily sprain an ankle or break a leg. And a dancer who is stomping it up is not likely to be on the lookout for holes in the ground.

The perfect dance area must have shade. The best kind is the dance arbor. A favorite in the plains area where there aren't many shade trees, the dance arbor protects dancers from the sun.

Dance arbors vary in size and shape; the most common shape is circular, resembling a large doughnut. The area for dancing is in the unprotected "hole" of the doughnut; the outer rim affords shade for the spectators.

The dance arbor showing the inner and outer circle of uprights and crosspieces. Photograph taken while the Monroe Powwow arbor in Monroe, New York, was being built.

The Monroe Powwow dance arbor, viewed from the southeast. The doorway is at the far right.

Building the Dance Arbor

The size of the dance arbor should suit the number of dancers you want to accommodate. An arbor 100 feet in diameter will accommodate 500 to 600 dancers and several thousand spectators. The dance arbor — because of its circular shape — keeps everybody at the powwow together, with the focal point in the middle of the dance arbor.

To build the 100-foot dance arbor, you need posts ten feet high and 6 to 8 inches in diameter, and posts twelve feet high and the same diameter. Ideally, the posts should be made from ash and forked at the top. If ash is not available, use any kind of hardwood.

To lay out the "doughnut," first drive a stake in what will be the approximate center of the dancing area. This stake will later be replaced with the center pole or flagpole.

Close-up of the singer's stall, located in the first 10-foot square north of the doorway. The top is covered with a canvas tarp.

Round house used for indoor dances by Osage Indians. Photo taken in 1899 near the present site of Pawhuska, Oklahoma. (Photo: courtesy of Museum of the American Indian, Heye Foundation.)

Use a guide rope about fifty-one feet long. Make a lariat loop or slip knot at one end, and loop it over the center stake. Make one mark on the rope forty feet from the stake, and another fifty feet from the stake. The forty-foot mark represents the inside circle of uprights; the fifty-foot mark, the outer circle. The ten feet between these two marks later becomes shaded area.

Stretch the guide rope toward the east, and mark the "doorway."

Stretch the guide rope tight, from the center stake to the outer circle. Using a carpenter's rule or a ten-foot board, make marks in the ground ten feet apart around the inner circle (at the forty-foot mark on the guide rope). Also mark the place for the corresponding upright around the outer circle (at the fifty-foot mark on the guide rope). The distance between uprights in the outer circle will be slightly greater than ten feet.

When all of the marks have been made, dig a two-foot hole at each mark. The twelve-foot uprights are placed in the holes in the inner circle, and the ten-foot uprights are placed in the outer circle. When the uprights are in place and the holes filled in with rocks and dirt, the uprights around the inner circle will be ten feet above ground and those around the outer circle will be eight feet above ground.

Next, connect all of the inner uprights together, and all of the outer uprights together by laying eleven-foot saplings from upright to upright.

112

You now have two rough concentric circles formed from the joined uprights. Now lay eleven-foot saplings across from the inner to the outer circles and four to five feet apart. Over this framework of saplings lay foliage (pine is preferred). Sometimes whole saplings with the leaves left on are laid across the crosspieces.

Rope off or board off the first ten-foot-square section north of the arbor for exclusive use by the singers and master of ceremonies. If a public-address system is used, it should be placed in this area so that both the master of ceremonies and singers may control it.

All dancers enter the dance arbor through the doorway. During their rest periods they sit on benches placed under the shaded area near the singers. The dancing is done in the center of the arbor under open sky, while the spectators watch from under the shaded area. Usually spotlights are placed around the arbor to light the dance area at night.

Dancing Indoors

The ideal indoor dance hall may be a basketball court, or any auditorium-like room that has a wooden floor. Avoid dancing on concrete, it is harmful to your feet and legs.

Many Indian winter powwows are conducted in frame houses especially built for community meetings and dances.

XXI

How to Run a Powwow

An Indian powwow produces a delicious assortment of wild scents: red-willow tobacco smoked by the old-timers, cooking fires off to the sides of the flapping four-walled tents and tipis, and Indian powder paint, sage, sweetgrass, and perfume.

The Indian powwow is also a conglomeration of exotic sounds: the voices of the singers, the clanging of the dancers' bells, the pulsation of the dance drum, the underlying murmur, of the spectator applause, the bark of a dog, and the vibrating tremolo of happy women's voices.

And what sights! The young dancers in their feathered costumes. The women in their buckskin dresses and fringed shawls. The grandmothers in simple ankle-length cotton dresses, heavily sequined shawls, and plain boot-moccasins. The old men in once colorful but now faded shirts, nodding their wispy, graying braids in silent approval of the day's showing of dancers.

And everyone mills about the dance arbor, visiting friends, running after near-lost children. Tubfuls of hot dogs in boiling water. And the ever-present favorite, cherry pop. And spectators, tired from long journeys to the powwow, sitting in their dusty cars simply looking on.

At hobbyist powwows, much of the same atmosphere prevails. To ensure success for your powwow, the physical arrangements and program must be carefully planned.

The Committee

A committee should be appointed to arrange the powwow, hire the singers, invite the dancers, and publicize the event. All aspects of the powwow should be carefully studied: the camping

114

Tipis at the 1964 Monroe Powwow. Tipis provide atmosphere and make good dressing rooms and sleeping quarters. These tipis were made by the Indian-lore camp staff of the Farm and Wilderness Camps at Woodstock, Vermont.

facilities, parking, tickets (if admission is to be charged) contests, and prizes. Preferably one person should be placed in charge of each of these responsibilities.

There should also be a master of ceremonies who is responsible for conducting the powwow program. It will be his duty to announce the powwow dances and specialty numbers, and to continuously encourage everyone to dance. He should explain each dance to the novices and spectators. A good master of ceremonies can greatly enhance your powwow and stimulate the singers and dancers into having a better time.

The Singers

Nowadays it is possible to hire Indian singers for your powwow. Many Indians live in metropolitan areas and have their own Indian dance clubs. Indian singers and specialty dancers should be payed and their room and board arranged.

Grass dance of the Crow Indians. This photo was taken around 1880-1890 in Montana Territory. (Photo: courtesy of Museum of the American Indian, Heye Foundation.)

Singers and dancers can also be hired from reservations. Contact must be made with the tribal councils of the reservations. Most of the tribal councils can be reached by writing to the Indian agency. Many of these agencies are marked on good state maps. The U.S. Bureau of Indian Affairs, Washington, D.C., provides a map of all Indian reservations and communities in the United States.

Schedule

Most powwows are on weekends. Dancers arrive Friday night or early Saturday morning and set up their campsites. The bulk of the program is on Saturday afternoon and evening, and Sunday morning.

The program officially opens Saturday morning after breakfast with the raising of the flag and an invocation. If Indians are present, chances are they will have an appropriate flag-raising song to sing.

After flag raising, the powwow begins. Usually eight or ten war-dances of various tempos are sung, interrupted by round dances and two-steps.

After lunch, the powwow begins again. The junior dance contests are usually held in the afternoon. Also there are specialty dances, and a host of war-dances. The flag is lowered at dusk.

At night, there are more specialty dances, and the senior war-dance contests are held. There are always proportionately more round dances and rabbit dances at night. When the dancers tire, they change back into their street clothes. They come back to the dance area to dance more round dances, rabbit dances, and now, the forty-nines and stomp dances.

On Sunday, the routine of flag raising is repeated, and war-dances, round dances and two-steps are danced until the powwow comes to a close. The flag is then lowered in mid-afternoon.

Opening and Closing the Ceremonies

At many powwows, the evening session begins with a procession of all participants. Some dance clockwise, and others dance counterclockwise. They meet in the center, and then they break into a fast war-dance. In Indian processional dances, veterans always lead the rest of the group.

There is a beautiful way of closing each powwow session called "singing the dancers off." This is usually done by the Sioux of South Dakota and may take place before lunch, before dinner, and before the last dance of the evening. For the last dance, the singers take their place next to the flagpole. They begin the song, and the dancers dance up to them, moving tightly around the singers. As the singers finish each chorus of the song, they begin walking toward the doorway of the dance arbor. They walk slowly for one chorus of the song, and then they stand in place for another chorus. This continues until the dancers are "sung off" the dance area. The last song may last fifteen or twenty minutes. On some occasions, I have seen singers in South Dakota lead the dancers right to their camps.

Holding the Give-away

A popular part of any powwow is the give-away. This is a traditional ceremony among American Indians when one person wishes to honor another, either living or dead, by giving away a gift.

In the olden days horses, tipis, and food were the customary gifts. Today, it is usually money that is given away, but occasionally an Indian will present you with a painted stick, which means that he is offering you a meal. On the appointed day, you take the stick to his house, and he fulfills his obligation by feeding you.

When giving-away, the usual procedure is to tell the master of ceremonies that you wish to give away something (money, a piece of Indian craftwork, and so on). You tell him to whom the gift is being given, and in whose memory it is being given. Then you must also give-away to the singers. On Indian reservations, the singers are "paid" this way.

After you have told the master of ceremonies your intention, he announces it in a loud, clear voice for everyone to hear. When the recipient of the gift hears his name, he comes forward and shakes your hand, shakes the hand of the master of ceremonies, and receives the gift.

When the singers hear that they are receiving a donation, the lead singer approaches, shakes the hand of the donor, and shakes the hand of the master of ceremonies. The singers then return to the drum and sing either a song in honor of the person you wished remembered (if he is dead) or a song using your name (if you have an Indian name) telling what a generous person you are.

This is an age-old custom among many Indian tribes and one that is very popular today. A man could always show his generosity and charity by giving-away at the powwows.

When the singers sing the give-away song, you and the person to whom you have given-away, dance alone for the first song, after which all of the dancers join in.

Much of the intermission time is taken up by trading for handicraft articles. At many powwows, Indian craftsmen are invited to set up booths and sell their wares to spectators and hobbyists. Other Indians sell various assortments of Indian foods, all of which adds wonderful atmosphere to any powwow. Hobbyists may spread blankets on which they exhibit their handicraft articles. At some larger powwows, craftwork is displayed in special halls. Prizes may be awarded for the best craft displays.

Paul Armstrong, president of the New Jersey Homecoming Powwow, acts as master of ceremonies during a give-away. He is wearing a modern northern-style grass-dance costume.

Good time — Indian time

There is a phenomenon among American Indians (and hobbyists) called *Indian time*. Indian time is a total disregard for clocks, watches, and time in general. Most powwows are run on Indian time. It is good to note that when you visit Indians, their activities will run about one to two hours behind the scheduled time. Sometimes notices and invitations to powwows are sent out with the words *Indian time* written at the bottom. Indian time has one advantage: you're hardly ever late for powwow!

XXII

Sources of Information

To help you learn more about Indian dancing, singing, and costume-making, the following sources are recommended.

Indian Dancing

The ideal way to learn Indian dancing is from the Indians themselves. If you live near a reservation or near an Indian community, it will be easy to strike up an acquaintance with an Indian family, who will be more than glad to teach you.

There are a few books on Indian interpretative dancing. Though they lack authenticity, they are good for programs for children in the Cub Scouts and Y.M.C.A. Guides. The most popular is *Dances and Stories of the American Indian,* by Bernard S. Mason. Another is *Rhythm of the Red Man,* by Julia M. Buttree.

Indian Music

Three companies in the United States provide most of the recorded Indian music:

(1) American Indian Soundchief, 1415 Carlson Drive, Klamath Falls, Oregon, specializes in northern- and southern-plains-Indian music.

(2) Canyon Records, 834 North 7th Avenue, Phoenix, Arizona.

(3) Folkways Records, 165 West 46th Street, New York, New York.

Records produced by these companies may be ordered directly (catalogs are available) or from Indian suppliers.

There are no popular books written on Indian music, but some technical books do exist. The best works are by Frances Densmore (Bulletins of the Bureau of American Ethnology). Her best books are *Teton Sioux Music, Chippewa Music* (in two volumes), and a series of smaller works on Pawnee Menominee, Ute, and Papago music. They may be found in many reference libraries.

Costume-Making

Here are two good books on costume-making for beginners:

(1) *The Book of Indian Crafts and Indian Lore,* by Julian Harris Salomon.

(2) *The Book of Indian Crafts and Costumes,* by Bernard S. Mason.

Advanced students of Indian costuming usually inspect museum specimens to learn how they are made. Devoted craftsmen use only those raw materials that were available to the American Indian before the arrival of the Whiteman. Many hobbyists are master "artifakers."

Indian Suppliers

Plume Trading and Sales Company has been the largest supplier of American Indian materials since 1927. (Office and mail-order division: P.O. Box 585, Monroe, New York.) A catalog is available. James M. Luongo, president, has one of the finest Indian collections in the country housed in the Plume Indian Museum.

Another favorite supplier of hobbyists is Grey Owl Indian Craft Manufacturing Company, 150-02 Beaver Road, Jamaica, New York. A catalog is available upon request.

There are many arts-and-crafts shops on Indian reservations. A map of these reservations may be obtained from the U.S. Bureau of Indian Affairs, Washington, D.C.

Literature

There are thousands of books about American Indians. Many are listed in the suppliers' catalogs. The University of Oklahoma's *Civilization of the American Indian* series is one of the most comprehensive collections. Advanced students usually turn to the annual reports and bulletins of the Bureau of American Ethnology in Washington, D.C. Others carefully study the bulletins of universities and museums.

A newsletter called *Powwow Trails* keeps hobbyists informed of powwows and other Indian activities. It may be ordered from Box 268, Somerset, New Jersey. It's objectives are to promote attendance at American Indian and hobbyist powwows and encourage the sale of Indian arts and crafts.

Historical Societies

A complete listing of historical societies is available from the American Association for State and Local History, 151 East Gorham Street, Madison, Wisconsin. Many of these societies publish periodicals that contain excellent information on Indians.

Museums

There are many fine Indian museums throughout the country. Of special interest to hobbyists are the Heye Foundation (Museum of the American Indian), and the American Museum of Natural History, both in New York City; the Peabody Museum at Harvard University; the Field Museum in Chicago; and the Denver Art Museum. In Anadarko, Oklahoma, thousands of visitors flock to Indian City, U.S.A., which contains authentic reproductions of Indian dwellings. In states where there are large Indian populations, many smaller museums can be found along the highways.

Index

accents, 21
All American Indian Days, 12
American Indian Exposition, 12, 88
aprons, 104
Arapaho, 26, 42, 57
arms, 27-29

Basic Body Movements, 23-29
Basic Steps, 30-35
bells, 104, 106
Blackfeet, 57, 60
Blood, 57
body positions, 53-55
boraches, 18
Boy Scouts, 79
breechcloth, 104-105
Buffalo dance, 21, 84-87
Bureau of Indian Affairs, 116
bustle, 104, 106

Cheyenne, 26, 42, 57
Chippewa, 12, 17, 57
closing ceremony, 117
Comanche, 13, 42, 57
contests, 60-62
costumes, 61-62, 67, 71, 74, 80, 83, 87,
    94-95, 102-108, 121
Cree, 21, 26, 60, 68
Creek, 88
cross-over, 38, 40, 52
Crow, 12, 21, 72, 116

Crow Indian Fair, 12

dance arbor, 109-113
dance area, 109
dance club, 15
dance drum, 18
dance team, 15
drag step, 53
drumming, 17-22, 58-59, 63, 65, 68,
    72, 74-76, 78, 80-81, 86-88, 97
drums, 18-19
drumsticks, 19

Fancy Dancing, 42-45
Fancy Dance Variation, 46-55
Flag dance, 75-76
flutes, 18
Fort Qu'Appelle, 12
Forty-nine, 13, 21, 65-67, 95
Frontier Days, 13

give-away, 117-118
Grass dance, 57, 116

hair roach, 103-105
half-time, 21
hand drums, 19
hands, 27-28
head dancer, 60
head movements, 25-28
historical societies, 122

Hobby, the, 14
hoop, 97
Hoop dance, 96-102
hop-turns, 46-53, 55
How to Run a Powwow, 114-119

Indian hobbyist, 14
Indian Lore, 14
Indian time, 119
Inter-Tribal Ceremonial, 12
Iroquois, 12

jarring, 36-38

Kiowa, 13, 42, 57

legs, 35
literature, 121-122
Little Big Horn, 11

master of ceremonies, 115, 118-119
Mesquakie, 12, 62, 80
Mesquakie Indian Powwow, 12
moccasins, 104
Monroe Powwow, 15-16, 99, 110, 115
museums, 122

National Anthem, 76
Navajo, 17
New Jersey Indian Homecoming Pow-
    wow, 19, 61, 119

Old-time Dancing, 36-41
Omaha dance, 57
Omaha Indian, 57
one-quarter time, 20
one-string violin, 18
opening ceremony, 117
Order of the Arrow, 79
Osage, 13, 57, 112
Oto, 13, 42, 55, 57

"Pan-Indian," 58
Pawnee, 13, 57

Pendleton Roundup, 13
pivots, 51
Ponca, 13, 42, 57
posture, 23-24
Potawatomi, 108
powwow, 14-15
powwow circuit, 13
powwow committee, 114-115
powwow dance, 57
powwow schedule, 116-117
processional, 77
Pueblo, 12, 17, 96
push-turns, 38

quick-steps, 51-52

Rabbit dance, 13, 21
rattles, 18
Red-and-White dance, 71
rhythm, 20-21
Round dance, 13, 21, 63-65
round house, 112
Ruffle dance, 74

Scout dance, 72
Seminole, 17, 88
shield, 80
Shield dance, 78
Shoshone, 57, 72
shoulders, 26
side-to-side, 53
singers, 17-18, 56, 115-116, 118
singers' costumes, 108
singing, 17-22, 58-59, 63-64, 66, 69,
    71-78, 81, 86, 88, 90-95, 97, 120-121
Sioux, 11-12, 16-19, 21, 23, 26, 56-57,
    60, 68, 71-72, 74-77, 80, 85, 106-
    107, 117
Sioux Sun dance, 12
Snake dance, 81-83
Sneak-up dance, 21, 72-74
Sources of Information, 120-122
spear, 80
Stomp dance, 88-95

Straight dance, 57
style, 29
suppliers, 121

tail, 60
tail dancer, 60
tap-heel, 37-38
tap-step, 31-33, 42-44, 50-51, 53
Teguia, 81
tempo, 20-21
three-quarter time, 20-21
thunder drumming, 21
toe-heel, 34-35

torso, 27
trading, 118
"tricks," 55
trots, 40
Two-step, 68

War dance, 20, 56-62
whistles, 18
Winnebago, 105-106, 108
Wisconsin Dells, 12
Wolf dance, 57
women's costume, 107-108
Wounded Knee, 11

The Author

WILLIAM K. POWERS has spent 16 years researching American Indian dance, music, and language. Specializing in Sioux, he was adopted by them and given the Indian name, Wanbli Waste (Good Eagle). The author was formerly an associate editor of *American Indian Tradition* magazine and now publishes a newsletter for Indian hobbyists. When the family is not following the powwow circuit, they make their home in Kendall Park, New Jersey. Son, Jeffrey, known as Wicahpi Ska (White Star), is already a champion dancer at age five.